PSYCHIC
SENSE

A REALISTIC APPROACH TO
DEVELOPING YOUR OWN PSYCHIC POWERS

PSYCHIC SENSE

ANDREW FITZHERBERT

ANGUS
& ROBERTSON
PUBLISHERS

For my wife, Gale,
without whom this book
would not have been written.

ANGUS & ROBERTSON PUBLISHERS

Unit 4, Eden Park, 31 Waterloo Road,
North Ryde, NSW, Australia 2113, and
16 Golden Square, London W1R 4BN,
United Kingdom

First published in Australia
by Angus & Robertson Publishers in 1986
First published in the United Kingdom
by Angus & Robertson (UK) Ltd in 1986
Reprinted 1986

Copyright © Andrew Fitzherbert 1986

National Library of Australia
Cataloguing-in-publication data.

Fitzherbert, Andrew, 1949-   .
    Psychic sense.

    ISBN 0 207 15218 7.

    1. Psychical research. 1. Title.

133.8

Typeset in 10pt Trump Mediaeval
Printed in Australia by
The Dominion Press–Hedges & Bell

CONTENTS

Chapter One
PSYCHIC READERS:
THE GOOD, THE NOT-SO-GOOD
AND THE TERRIBLE

The best psychic reader I ever encountered was a little Hungarian man who worked with a tattered deck of gypsy cards. The first time I met him he told me about my mother, my brothers, my children, my brother's children, my wife, my wife's family and, of course, about myself. If this sounds unbelievable, I could hardly believe it myself at the time. Louie Olah was not just psychic: he was incredibly, extraordinarily psychic. And Louie was not a high-priced society clairvoyant catering to media megastars. He was a small-time psychic reader working from a tea lounge in Australia.

Psychical research has always fascinated me. From my childhood in the semi-desert outback of Queensland, I have travelled to all the cities of Australia, then on to England, Canada and the United States. I have lived and worked on three continents and made visits to Singapore, India and elsewhere. During my travels I continually sought out occult societies and psychic groups, meeting and talking with practising occultists and psychics. Slowly over the years I learned to unfold my own latent psychic abilities. Since 1970, when I made my first faltering attempts to "sense" things psychically, I have gone on to give public demonstrations of clairvoyance, prediction and telepathy. I have presented private displays of almost every type of psychic ability, with the sole exception of the so-called "physical phenomena" which are not within my power.

You too can learn to do these things. Here in this book I have set out a method to teach you to develop your psychic powers. And none of it will be by magic spells, mystic prayers or wild guesswork, nor methods copied out of old books which have never worked and never will work. The methods herein are ones that I know will work, for these are the methods I have used with great success myself.

Before we begin there is one thing that must be made clear: the psychic scene is riddled with fraud, delusion, false hopes and all types of misleading ideas. For every good psychic I have met there are a dozen who think they are psychic but who are really self-deluded, and three or four con artists who pull "psychic tricks" in order to relieve you of your money. Good psychics are as rare as diamonds. First-class psychics are found as often as 100-carat rubies. If you want to be psychic yourself, you will have to avoid all the traps. And you will have to work at it because psychic powers, like muscles, can only be developed with a lot of effort.

To illustrate just what sort of results you can expect, let us have a look at some actual psychic readers and what they do. Louie, the Hungarian card-reader, was brought to my attention by many people I had met who had extraordinary stories about the man. Some people reported that his predictions had come true under the most unlikely circumstances, while other predictions that had failed nevertheless "fitted in" with the goings-on in those people's lives at the time. I heard so many tall tales that I decided to try a private reading with Louie. When I telephoned for an appointment I was pleasantly surprised that he did not ask my name, but simply entered me as "a gentleman, two o'clock Thursday".

His office was a small shop in a back street of the city with a sign on the door reading "Personal Horoscopes". This did not look promising since card-reading has nothing to do with casting horoscopes. Later I learned that Louie's command of written English was not sufficient for him to realise that he had the wrong word on his door. On entering, I found half the shop was partitioned into a waiting-room while the other half had a desk and two chairs for Louie and his client.

After a few moments Louie invited me to sit down. He was a small man, his face twisted and scarred from old war injuries. He worked with quick, nervous words and gestures. I was asked to cut and shuffle the deck of cards, which he then spread on the desk. He picked them up one at a time as he worked. One thing immediately apparent to me was that Louie took very little notice of the cards. He would pick up one or two cards, glance absent-mindedly at them and then launch into some complicated statement which could have no relation whatsoever to the piece of painted cardboard.

"First, I will ask you some simple questions, but you tell me only yes or no, OK?" he announced. I nodded in reply. "You are married, yes?" he asked.

"Yes," I replied.

"And you have two children, yes?" he went on.

This was a poser. I have no children of my own, but living with me were my wife's young daughter and her teenaged sister, very much like my own two kids. So I told him, "Yes", to this.

"They are both girls and one is teenage," he said with no hesitation. Now that was good. So I told him who the two girls were. He then described their character, talents and probable futures with alarming accuracy.

"Your mother is alive, yes?"

"That's right."

"But your father is dead."

"Yes."

He went on to tell me that my mother lived alone, in a small town, and he described her work in the Country Women's Association.

"You have two brothers."

"Yes."

"They all live different cities. One brother is married with two children. Other brother not married. He wears uniform. Is religious man."

And so it went on. My wife was from overseas, her parents are separated, her siblings are so-and-so, her father lives near her, etcetera. One by one, Louie covered everybody related to me, making comments on their lives and predicting something of their future. In every case, his descriptions were deadly accurate.

It was curious that in all this mass of information there was very little that applied directly to me or my personal life. Louie was unable to discern my job though he correctly stated that I worked alone and helped people. He made a few predictions about travel and success in my future and other long-term predictions that will take me decades to see out. Though information on my own life was skimpy, as a display of psychic ability Louie's reading was absolutely outstanding. How could anyone possibly reel off so many private and pertinent facts about the family of a total stranger?

It is now several years since this reading took place, and in fact some of Louie's predictions have not worked out. A few have proved true, others may come about in the future. But Louie's description of my family members was a first-rate experience which I have not encountered with a psychic since. He himself admits that his predictions are variable — hundreds of people have been given details about their own futures which did indeed occur, while others report "near misses" or total failure. This brings us to a most important point which all psychics should clearly understand. This is that the future is not something fixed and unchangeable, so that a psychic preview of the future may or may not prove to be true. However, psychic perception properly applied can give fantastic insight into things as they are and can often give a glimpse of things as they will be. Psychic awareness is an invaluable and powerful tool for those who have developed it, but it needs to be treated with care.

Louie is the best of the psychic readers I have encountered, but I have met many others who do excellent work. From my files I can find hundreds of cases of predictions that came about and descriptions that were totally accurate. There was the street psychic in India many years ago who casually told me the date and circumstances of my future marriage. There was the Spiritualist in England who described the house where we would first stay in Canada. No fewer than four Canadian psychics predicted the cancellation of an overseas business trip which would be postponed to a later date, at a time when the first arrangements had not even been made for this trip. Both the cancellation and later completion of the trip occurred as predicted.

I have given public displays of ESP and in every case I scored a high rate of success. But these success stories are only part of the picture. There are far more cases of unsuccessful psychics and dishonest pseudopsychics than there are cases of genuine ESP. Let me describe some of the not-so-good psychic readers.

Herman Van Dyke (not his real name) calls himself a clairvoyant. He never bothers to advertise because enough clients return to him on a regular basis for him to be continually booked ahead. He uses no cards or other tools, but merely sits with a client and tells him or her whatever comes into his head. Here is a transcript of one of his tape-recorded readings:

"You know, as soon as you came in, I picked up the impression of worry. Now why are you worried?"

The client replied non-committally that she had no idea. She was not worried.

"Well, there is someone around you who is worried? A woman?"

"There are plenty of worried people around me. I know lots of people."

"Well, let it go. You seem to be very busy at present and I feel very excited with what you're doing. It's as if everything is starting to pay off for you. France, I get France. Now why is this?"

"I sent a letter to a friend in France yesterday," replied the client.

"That's it then. Who's Bob? Or Robert?"

"There's a Robert where I work."

"I don't trust it. I don't get a good feeling about him. You know, you will go on a trip later this year which will be very good for you. Who do you know that drives a grey car?"

"I don't know anyone who does."

"Well, there is a grey car. Keep it in mind. You know, there's someone around you who is very sophisticated. Do you know her?"

"Yes, I think so."

"Well, she's going from the frypan right into the fire. I don't feel good with her at all."

And so he went. About half of what he said had no relevance to the client at all, while the whole reading was so general it might have applied to anyone. And yet the client was satisfied that Herman had genuine ability. The remark about France had seemed relevant; she did have a sophisticated sister who is forever in predicaments, and Robert, the man at work, was dying of cancer. So although none of Herman's comments was specifically accurate and may have been guesses, there does seem to be a trace of ESP at work with this man.

Herman's readings are quick and lively and he encourages his clients to talk to him. Many people go to psychics to talk out their problems so a sympathetic reader will always have a certain number of clients. With a lot of talking and a little ESP plus a pleasant manner, Herman Van Dyke has built himself a solid reputation. His actual psychic ability is that of the gypsy tearoom reader, but he manages to present himself as something better.

Herman is a Dutchman, and as another example of not-so-good psychism, let us look at another Dutch clairvoyant currently working in New York. We shall call him William Noom to protect his identity. William has a thriving business owing to frequent appearances at parties and social affairs where he entertains the guests with his ESP. His private readings are always well patronised. William is small, excitable and quick of speech which makes him entertaining whether he uses ESP or not. He once singled me out of a group of people at a public meeting where he was giving a demonstration.

"You, sir!" he called out. "Can you hear me?"

"I hear you William!" I shouted so everyone could hear.

"You're the real life of the party, aren't you?" he shot back. "You can go places and get everyone talking at once. You really love to stir things up."

"That's right," I told him. "My wife says I do it too much, though!" Everyone laughed.

"You're going to get a promotion," said William.

"Can't," I told him. "I'm self-employed."

"Well, your business is going to take off then. Your wife does your books for you, doesn't she?"

"That's right."

"She's a really good organiser, much better than you, sir. You do the work but she organises you." There was more laughter and I told him that he was right. "Oh, and you're going to the optometrist soon," he added. "I can see you sitting in the optometrist's chair."

A month later, I did indeed visit the optometrist for a new pair
of glasses under orders from my wife who hated my old
spectacles. Now this looks as though William was completely
right on the four points he made to me. But think it over. I was
wearing a bright red shirt and answered him in a loud voice
which was a good clue to his "life-of-the-party" comment. I
myself told him that I was self-employed and had a wife, and
many such men do have wives who like to organise them. I also
had taken my glasses off and put them on again several times that
evening which was the perfect clue about the optometrist.

So was William really psychic or merely very quick to pick up
clues? I have listened to William Noom reading for several people
and I noticed that with all of them much of his information stems
from the person's appearance, manner and speech. Every so often
he would dramatically make a prediction and, by reputation,
these predictions are usually accurate. But they are filled out by
much that is probably not psychic at all.

William Noom is not a fraud. When he tells a businessman
with worn shoes that he has been having financial problems
lately, he is not consciously faking. He genuinely gets an
impression of tight finances but it is not coming from his ESP.
Rather it comes from the observation that wealthy men do not
wear worn shoes. If he stopped to analyse the impression he
would realise it himself, but William never stops. He just rattles
along with whatever he "picks up" and somewhere in all of those
impressions there are always flashes of real psychic awareness.

Both William Noom and Herman Van Dyke present themselves well, which certainly helps their success. Occasionally an
outright fraud decides to turn to psychism as a means of money-
making. If the fraud is well presented he usually succeeds in
conning the public. But there are also plenty of untalented people
who think they are genuinely psychic. These are mainly concentrated in the Spiritualist churches.

Spiritualism as a method of psychical development is discussed
in Chapter Four of this book. The top Spiritualist mediums and
clairvoyants have always led the world in their public displays of
ESP. However, many Spiritualist churches are filled with silly
men and women who call themselves psychic but who are no
more psychic than a brick wall.

Hannah Bickerstaff, herself now dead, or "passed over" as the
Spiritualists say, was one of the first self-deluded psychic readers
I met. She was a tall, thin, dried-up old lady of kindly nature and
negligible education who regularly performed at a Spiritualist
church. She also conducted a small private psychic practice. Her
technique went like this: "With you, dear, I feel as if I were push-

ıg up a steep hill. You keep trying and trying but you never quite ɛt to the top. Sometimes you wonder whether it's all worth-hile, but then you go on again. You get depressed sometimes, ɔn't you? But you never give up. Well, the hill is becoming less eep. Over the next few weeks things will become better and ɔu'll be able to lift up your head and say, 'At last things are arting to work out'. Those dark clouds are starting to peel away ıd before long, you'll be stepping out with a light tread again."

Having delivered this encouraging nonsense to one listener, annah would then turn to the next church member. She would and silently for a moment, waiting for psychic impressions, and ıen off she would go once more: "I feel with you that there have ɛen restrictions. It's like being inside a box. There is no room to ıove. Whichever way you try to reach out, something stops you. 'hat you need to do is to break out of the box. Break through the alls of the box and you can set yourself free. You think that you ın't, but if you try you will find that you can. In just a few ɛeks, there will be an opportunity to strike out in a new rection, and if you seize it, you'll break out of that box and be ɛe."

Hannah could perform 20 of these inspiring messages in a half-ɔur and she firmly believed that they were all genuine psychic ıpressions. Presumably most of the people who came to see her so believed this. But, of course, there was nothing psychic ɔout her whatever. Unfortunately there are hundreds of annahs in the psychic field, churning out this drivel. The ınazing thing is that these people could easily develop genuine ɔychic ability if only they would set about it the right way.

Another technique used by many so-called psychics is stringing ɔgether a series of common names or common incidents which e bound to fit someone in the audience. The line "someone ɔives a grey car" is typical (you will remember that Herman Van yke used this one). A famous English spirit medium, Dora B., ɛes to pass into a trance and give inspired messages such as this: I get the name Mabel. And the name Fred. And someone called ɔbert. There's a lady who does sewing and a man who goes ɔhing. And someone who used to play the piano. And I get the tter 'J'. There's a woman who had a bad leg, does anyone know ɛr?" Dora usually gives each listener 10 minutes of this guff ɛfore pulling a few funny faces which she claims represent the ces of the spirits of the dead. People pay a fancy price to attend ɛr seances and yet there are thousands of genuine clairvoyant ɔiritualists turning out far better work than the famous Dora.

Among the fraudulent psychics, the con men who pretend to be airvoyant, two rules prevail: firstly, they advertise widely and

charge very high prices. Secondly, when a client arrives a way
found to fill in the duration of the consultation without actual
doing anything psychic. There are several ways in which fa
psychics do this. The most skilled of them have slick methods f
obtaining information or using clever generalisations — the so
of techniques used by stage magicians who specialise in "ment
magic" shows. Few con men, however, know more than one
two of these techniques. When professional magicians, like th
Amazing Randi, describe trick methods for appearing to l
psychic, they tell of techniques usually beyond the ability
most fake clairvoyants. Instead the frauds fill out a reading wi
flattery or philosophy and they keep clever conjuring to
minimum.

The flatterers simply tell the client how wonderful he or she
or how psychic he or she is or how successful he or she will be
the near future. Half an hour of marvellous predictions for gre
success will usually satisfy anyone and, in practice, a client wh
has been told he or she is a fine person who will soon be rich ar
famous will seldom notice that the clairvoyant has given n
indication of real psychic ability.

The philosopher cultivates an easy-going style, much like
doctor's bedside manner, and simply sits and talks with th
client. They talk about life and about psychic phenomena. The
offer a little homely advice about health and money and the
make a few vague predictions about nice things to come. At th
end of an hour, the client leaves with the impression that he ha
been listening to a kindly, sincere psychic, a really nice perso
He has few regrets about the money just spent. Of course, no
many of these clients will come back for more, but the fake clai
voyant merely keeps advertising and there will always be ne
clients turning up. A small number of simple-minded people wi
return to the fake who will quickly pick up through conversatio
enough about their lives to support a pretence of having re
psychic powers. With these and new clients the fake makes
living.

You may think that I have been exaggerating when I talk abou
the self-deluded pseudopsychics and the 100 per cent frauduler
ones. But in fact these people actually outnumber the ones wh
have any psychic ability at all. The whole business gets really
nasty when the fake clairvoyant decides to trick his or her client
out of large sums of money using any one of a dozen methods. H
or she may discover a "curse" on the unlucky client which wi
cost a small fortune to remove by magical means. He or she ma
tell the client about some marvellous way to make money whic
depends upon advancing $1000 to the clairvoyant. The police i

l big cities are familiar with these and similar devices. My own
es are filled with news clippings of duped people and fraudulent
airvoyants involved in such swindling.

You can read in books and magazines about the supposed
tars" of the psychic scene, the clairvoyants who pander to
ovie stars. Many of these are genuine psychics who have
anaged to contact the right clients and who receive enormous
blicity as a result. In fact the Hollywood clairvoyants are
ually "good" rather than "outstanding", since it is likely that
nbition and luck contributed to their being in the spotlight
ore than did raw talent.

I have known psychics in England (where psychism is often of a
ry high standard) who could run rings around the top-priced
merican professionals, yet who charged a paltry $6 for a reading
at would carry a $500 price tag in Hollywood. The greatest of
e world's superpsychics have seldom bothered with the film
orld. They cater to more important individuals: the political
d social leaders of the world. Certainly there are innumerable
ychics who never get into the limelight at all, but among what
ight be termed the cream of the world's psychics it is in politics
ther than the theatre or film scene that they make their mark.

Many of these people are well known to historians and have
en the subject of books themselves. Cagliostro, who helped lay
e groundwork of the French Revolution, and St Germaine, who
ok part in the rearrangement of the monarchy of Russia in the
ne of Catherine the Great, are two examples of persons whose
ychic abilities alone garnered them the power they enjoyed. Let
e tell about one more, a man who died in 1936 in an American
reet and who had influenced the highest people in the world
lely by the public use of his clairvoyant ability.

Born in Ireland in 1866, the man became known as a brilliant
ychic in London during the 1880s. By 1910 he had worked for
l the members of the British royal family except Queen
ctoria; become a spy for the British government for missions in
ussia, Germany and France; engineered a political treaty
tween France and England (the Entente Cordiale); worked for
sorted American governors and other politicians; taken part in
e "Troubles" in Ireland at the highest political level; and had
unded two newspapers, a bank and a champagne business. As
intelligence agent he played a significant part in the Russian
volution, the Sino-Japanese War and the First World War. All of
is was done on the strength of an outstanding clairvoyant
ility which brought him fame, money and prestige. The man in
estion was Count Louis Hamon, known to the public under his
n-name of "Cheiro". He wrote a score of books, including his

own memoirs, but the truth about this remarkable man is not t be found in any of them. Count Hamon did far more than he eve thought fit to include in his books, but silence is an invaluabl virtue in a clairvoyant who works for governments.

I do not claim to be as psychic as Count Louis Hamon. Thi man was born with a strong psychic gift and worked hard t develop it further. Nor do I ever do psychic readings for the publi in a professional way. My own career keeps me busy enough and have no desire to set up as a professional psychic reader. Some times I have volunteered my services for psychic demonstration often I make psychic comments for friends or people I meet; and of course, I use ESP in my private life, though not as often as yo might think. Intelligence, knowledge, experience, work and con monsense are all equally useful for everyday living, and whil ESP is a nice thing to have it is by no means the answer to life every dilemma.

This book is intended to guide those people who would like t develop their own latent psychic ability. When I first becam interested in psychic matters as a boy, I had no trace of psychi awareness at all. For years I studied and explored, read books an built up a private library (now numbering over 4000 volumes) c rare scholarly books on psychic subjects. People started to ask m whether I was psychic myself, and always I would answer "No"

It was not for lack of trying! I attended seances, learned t meditate, attended psychic classes and studiously read every thing I could on psychic development. I cast spells, bought a taro pack, learned hypnotism and carried out the exercises recom mended by a variety of occult teachers. There were many many exciting experiences along the way, but I never develope any psychic powers.

Then one day in 1970 someone introduced me to a minor psy chic game, just for a bit of fun. For a serious occultist such as considered myself to be, it seemed a foolish thing to do. But tried it . . . and it worked. It worked so well that I played th game again and it worked even better. I devised ways to improv the game and it worked better still. I told a friend, who replied "Well, then you must be psychic".

"Oh, no, I'm not!" I told her.

"Oh, yes you are," she argued. And she gave me a test, askin me to guess something. I concentrated for a minute and a answer floated into my mind. The right answer! I was psychi after all!

I practised and practised, learning more and practising mor and eventually I began to get good results indeed. I found that could do all sorts of psychic things besides the ordinary psychi feats. Let me list what I can do, and what I can teach you to do

1. Pick up facts about a person's home, life, work, family, etcetera.
2. Predict future events for people.
3. Predict world events and important happenings.
4. Diagnose certain health problems.
5. Pick up impressions of past incarnations for people, impressions that can be confirmed through historical studies or by other means.
6. Obtain information about the spirits of people who have died.
7. Sense and describe the past history of objects, buildings, etcetera.
8. Find lost objects.
9. Obtain things I want by psychically knowing where to get them.

In addition I can create impressions on objects or places that influence those who encounter them and sometimes influence the course of events. Despite my psychic abilities, however, I am never 100 per cent accurate or, rather, seldom so. There are times when every impression I have is correct but there are also times when I have been 100 per cent wrong. Let me give two examples to illustrate this.

My sister-in-law once asked me about the morals of a man who had just become her landlord. She was renting a section of his apartment. My impressions, given quickly, were these: he is completely disinterested in you and will give you no trouble at all. He has a stereo set that he is inordinately proud of. He is untidy and has messy habits, a typical bachelor. His two eyes are different. Then I described her apartment. I proved to be correct on every point and some six months later my sister-in-law commented that a photograph of this man showed one of his eyes to be much larger than the other, something she had never noticed when just looking at him.

The other story concerns two young sisters who were staying with my wife and me on their way to a European holiday. I spent an hour with them before they left, giving impressions of their coming trip. Ten days after their departure they abruptly cancelled the entire holiday and returned home, thus disproving all of my predictions. What happened? Why should endless cases of predictions prove true while this set of predictions was so wrong? I think the answer lies in the fact that one decision on the part of the two girls changed the entire pattern of their future. Had they gone on with the trip no doubt more would have been fulfilled. Of course there may be other explanations as well, but the point of the story is that no psychic impression is infallible. You must remember that point in all your dealings with psychic matters.

In Chapter Three I shall begin to tell you exactly how you can go about developing your psychic powers. But first we must have a chapter on the theory behind psychic development. The method is simple, so simple that I want you first to look at all the complexities which lie behind the subject before enjoying the actual experience.

Chapter Two
BASIC PRINCIPLES OF PSYCHIC DEVELOPMENT

This chapter is designed specifically for those who want to know the "how" and the "why" behind psychic development. You may be impatient to get to the actual methodology, but it is always better to know why you are doing something than just to follow instructions blindly. Many of the gurus and founders of psychic schools claim to have inspiration from higher sources or ancient wisdom so that the learner is told not to question what is taught. My own belief is that such teachers are just hiding their own inadequacies behind a screen and that everyone should be entitled to know the rationale for what they are asked to do or told to believe.

Several knowledgeable people have put forward theories about ESP, but most of these have proved to have little practical value. People often invent theories and then test them afterwards. My theories were developed to explain what had already been discovered through practical experience. Let us start with the obvious fact that human beings possess five senses: seeing, hearing, feeling, smelling and tasting. These senses date back to the earliest days of human evolution, though anthropologists and biologists believe that some of our senses are older than others. The sense of smell seems to have developed in the animal world before the sense of sight and, indeed, sight has been evolving steadily through the millennia so that modern humans see far better than their primitive ancestors could.

Besides the five senses people have always possessed an alternative means of gaining information, the "extrasensory" method. This special ability is not another sense, but an alternative to all the senses. It is something quite separate and apart from ordinary human senses and it is also something separate from the rational, logical parts of the mind. Extrasensory perception (ESP) is therefore not only distinct from the senses, it is also distinct from thinking and reasoning.

In a physical sense people were much the same 10,000 years ago as they are today. They are, of course, physically different from the prehuman ape-like creatures who preceded them a million or so years ago. However, the senses and the mind have not remained the same over those 10,000 years. People have come to depend more and more on the sense of sight and sense of

13

hearing to help them deal with the world and have hardly bothered with the sense of touch. The sense of taste and sense of smell have been positively neglected. People have also become increasingly dependent on rational thinking.

As civilisation became more complex, people used the reasoning parts of their minds more and more. Education, once enjoyed by less than one per cent of the population, is now available to all in western societies. Europeans, who before the twelfth century survived in simple farming communities, had progressed by the eighteenth century to the complexities of the Industrial Revolution with its greater demands on the mind. Now in the twentieth century nearly every child in western societies learns to read and the most rural-dwelling people enjoy a lifestyle incalculably more complex than their forefathers could have imagined. In short, people have evolved away from their extrasensory and extrarational abilities, and have become increasingly dependent on certain specialised senses along with the reasoning functions of the mind.

And yet there is evidence that a person's neglected senses can be tremendously developed if some effort is made to do so. Consider, for example, the sense of smell. To the modern western person, the sense of smell is mainly a source of pleasure, seldom a source of information. We enjoy the smell of food, amuse ourselves with perfumes and colognes and that is about it. Occasionally our nose sends us an important message: the gas is leaking, something is burning, this food is bad. Such messages may be invaluable once or twice a year or perhaps as rarely as once or twice in a lifetime. But generally the nose is not an important source of information.

There *are* people for whom the sense of smell is more important. For example, there are tribal people in the arid regions of Africa who can smell a waterhole 10 kilometres away. There are Aborigines living in Australia who can smell a man on horseback an hour before he rides into camp. Moreover, they can tell if he is black or white and, if he is a friend, they may recognise the man himself from his smell. There are reports of native sorcerers who can smell the fear on a guilty man.

And this is not all. We have gas-pipe workers who have trained themselves to smell a leak no ordinary human being could possibly detect. There are makers of perfume who can distinguish between thousands of subtle odours and blend them into exquisite and outlandishly expensive toiletries. These people have not neglected their sense of smell. They have developed it, utilised and refined it until their ability seems quite miraculous to those of us who have not tried. Here, then, we have proof that a neglected sense may be developed far beyond what would normally be the case.

Taste is another neglected sense. Yet here too we know that there are those who use it extensively. Wine-tasters, whisky-mixers and their fellow workers can perform the same miracles with their sense of taste as do the perfumers with their sense of smell. Could you distinguish between 120 different whisky flavours? There are people in Scotland who do this daily in the course of their work.

The sense of touch seems to lie halfway between the under-used senses of smell and taste and the more developed senses of sight and hearing. We use touch, yet it cannot be denied that people are capable of using it more than they do. The surgeon, the masseur, the raw-wool sorter: these are the experts who specialise and develop the touch sense. Nineteenth-century cardsharps worked with special cards so finely thinned that only a superfine sense of touch could detect the tampering. Perhaps they still do. Blind people working with braille depend on touch in order to read.

Clearly, then, people use some of their senses far more than others, though we have seen that the other senses are capable of being developed. We concentrate on certain senses simply because they are the most useful ones in our society. It is not a matter of laziness nor of prejudice: we utilise only what we need and simply disregard the rest.

Extrasensory perception (ESP) is not one of the senses but is a primitive alternative means for people to understand the environment. It is not nearly as effective as seeing and hearing, and for this reason people have never needed to develop it. If you work in an office it is far more effective to see, hear and touch everything in the room than to sit back and psychically "perceive" it all. In an evolutionary sense ESP, like the sense of smell, is simply not as useful as sight and hearing and consequently has been neglected.

You might think, then, that all that is necessary to develop your ESP is to practise and exercise it. Unfortunately this is not quite the case. Just as ESP is unconnected with the five senses on which we usually depend, it is also unconnected with the reasoning faculty of the mind on which we also depend. As long as people use their senses to perceive the world, they block out any latent ESP they may have. Just as surely, when they think and reason this too draws them further and further away from the use of ESP. Reason and the senses have developed together, while ESP has been left behind.

ESP is the primitive human method of perceiving the world. As long as a person uses his reason and employs his senses, this primitive method is prevented from functioning. We must do two things if we would regain the use of our psychic awareness: first, cut down our dependence on the senses, and second, close down the reasoning part of our minds. There is an obvious danger in such a programme: to abandon one's senses and one's mind is tantamount to abandoning one's sanity. It would give free play to fantasy and imagination, perhaps to illusions and hallucinations. If the thing is to be done we must find a way to close down the senses and the reason, yet maintain a firm grasp on reality. There must be a way to distinguish fantasy or imagination from genuine extrasensory perception.

I have given this paradox a name: "the believing–doubting tightrope". You have to "believe" in your extrasensory ability and at the same time "doubt" it (that is, test it to see if it is true). I call this a tightrope because obviously it is extraordinarily difficult to keep a balance between the two extremes. My theory states that ESP is a sort of primitive ability that evolved with the first of our senses, and has been virtually buried as people evolved along the path of reasoning and sensory awareness. If this theory is correct there should be evidence to support it. Also, the theory should be capable of being put to practical use. I believe this theory fulfils both conditions.

Extrasensory awareness has always been noted more in rural communities than in urbanised ones. Every known primitive tribe has its shaman, witchdoctor or magic man, many of whom have genuine ESP besides the usual bag of conjuring tricks such people employ. Similarly; throughout Europe and much of Asia it is the rural villages that have their witches or wise men. In the cities and metropolitan areas such natural psychics are seldom, if ever, found. The more primitive a culture, the more widespread the use of ESP. The more developed a culture becomes, the less ESP will be found in use. Does this not support the view that ESP is an essentially primitive ability?

If you interview the best professional psychics in the area where you live, you are sure to notice that one or two of the best are lacking in education, social skills and, sometimes, even literacy. Of course there are many who are not, but it is striking to discover that among the best psychic readers you will always find a number who are obviously very simple folk. One of the more amusing spectacles of the psychic scene is that of wealthy, cultured people riding in their expensive cars to call upon a shabby cottage where a toothless old crone will tell them their fortune. How have these folk who would seem to be the least fitted to succeed in modern society managed to secure the attention of the rich and famous? They are the natural psychics; the uneducated, uncultured minority in whom the extrasensory awareness has not been completely blocked out.

Another group among whom ESP is commonly found is children. Who has not met the harried mother who swears her baby screams whenever she tries to leave the house, even though the child is in another room and cannot possibly know what she plans? Colin Wilson, the distinguished author of *The Occult*, has an interesting theory that children learn to talk partly through the use of ESP. An observant parent will often note that a child seems to grasp the use of words and sentences not through studying how adults speak, but rather through a sort of instinctive awareness of their meaning. Psychologists seem to think that language is learned through a computer-like process going on in the child's mind. But no computer imaginable could do what every child does in a matter of two years.

Once a child has passed seven or eight years of age his or her ability to learn a language decreases. An adult with a highly trained mind may take years to master a language; how then does an infant manage this with no effort at all? The answer lies in the fact that the child's mind is not trained, nor is it cluttered with facts, ideas, opinions and the responsibilities of industrial living. In such a state the extrasensory ability is still present and the child benefits accordingly. The child literally "senses" the thoughts around it and in doing so soon learns to associate meaning with the words and sentences he or she hears.

Eileen Garrett, the brilliant British medium who collaborated for years with the world's best parapsychologists, notes in her book *Adventures in the Supernormal* that schizophrenics often show high levels of psychic awareness. As the schizophrenic approaches the point of total breakdown a flood of extrasensory impressions often flows into his or her mind. This observation has been confirmed by several psychologists working with schizophrenic patients, among them Dr Arthur Guirdham. What is happening in such cases is simply that the rational part of the mind is breaking down and, as it does so, it permits the usually suppressed psychic impressions to come pouring through. Unfortunately the schizophrenic is by this time so far out of touch with reality that he or she cannot make use of the ability he or she has unwittingly unleashed.

This evidence supports my theory that ESP is indeed a primitive human ability latent in all of us. But before exploring this further, let us take a look at some of the alternative theories that have been put forward from time to time. The biggest group of people ever to be concerned with psychic matters are the

Spiritualists. Spiritualism is a religious philosophy based on the belief that human beings live on after physical death and that it is possible to communicate with the spirits of the dead. Spiritualists believe that psychic impressions do not come from our own minds, but from the minds of disembodied spirits around us. Spiritualists are inclined to explain all psychic phenomena as the work of spirits. While few of them would deny that a person is capable of ESP on his own, most insist that psychic impressions are put into the mind by our spirit guides and are therefore not products of our own ability.

The Spiritualistic view is that when you die you pass on to the spirit world and that, in all probability, you continue to take an interest in still-living friends and relatives. Thus, when Great-aunt Mary, who baked fabulous biscuits, passes into the Great Beyond, she may well continue to supervise your own biscuit-baking from her new position in the spirit world. Spiritualism claims that all sorts of departed people may well be taking an interest in you, looking after your welfare and popping ideas into your mind whenever they get the chance. When you are asleep you are supposed to be particularly susceptible to picking up spirit messages and many dreams, it is said, are memories of genuine contact with the spirit world.

The Spiritualists' method of psychic development is to tune your mind in to the minds of the spirits, rather like tuning a radio to a particular station. This is done through prayer, meditation and "sitting in circles", which means joining a group of experienced mediums who are already in regular contact with the spirits. The circle is supposed to attract spirits like moths to a flame, so that the "developing" person will be more likely to pick up spirit messages.

If you happen to have no departed friends or relatives you can still expect to get help from the spirit world, as every person is said to have a number of spirit guides. These are miscellaneous spirits who have volunteered to look after you as a sort of public duty. (Whether they do so out of boredom, a love of supervising people or because you cannot look after yourself is never explained.)

Spiritualism is not a unified body, but contains thousands of independent churches, each with its own ideas. It is therefore unfair to say all Spiritualists believe such-and-such, but it is certainly true that most of them see ESP as a product of spirit help. There are Spiritualists who believe that people have their own extrasensory powers, but most persist in attributing their psychic impressions to the spirit world.

As was mentioned in Chapter One the religion is riddled with pseudopsychics of the Hannah Bickerstaff type: people who think they are psychic when in fact they are not. So although Spiritualism has produced some very fine psychics indeed, it is clearly not a reliable way to develop ESP. Further, the Spiritualist hypothesis is not adequate to explain the ordinary functioning of ESP. While it may well be true that spirits could influence human affairs, it is hard to believe that they are the only, or even the main, source of psychic impressions. There are plenty of successful psychics who have no belief in spirits at all yet who manage to do excellent work.

Before leaving Spiritualism I must mention one of the most famous books ever written on developing ESP. It is *Your Psychic Powers and How to Develop Them*, by Dr Hereward Carrington. Carrington was a famous psychical researcher who died in 1959 after writing more than 100 books on psychic subjects. Although he held critical attitudes to Spiritualism, Carrington wrote his most famous book from a Spiritualistic viewpoint. It is full of instructions on table-tipping, automatic writing, seances and other Spiritualist methods. Because the book is well written and Carrington was such a highly respected author, the book has always been much sought after. It is a convincing piece of work. But in one of his last books, *Psychic Oddities*, Hereward Carrington casually commented that he himself had absolutely no psychic ability! So his well-received book is totally theoretical as the author himself was unable to develop his own ESP.

Besides the Spiritualists there are at least two worldwide organisations that have specific views on psychic development. They are the Theosophical Society and the Ancient and Mystical Order of Rosae Crucis (AMORC), the largest and most influential of the Rosicrucian societies. AMORC teachings are available only to members and they will not be discussed here, though it is worth noting that AMORC's psychic techniques are only a part of a broad spectrum of self-development methods. However, the Theosophical theory of the nature of psychic phenomena deserves some attention. The Society was founded in 1875 by a group of people who had gathered around a remarkable Russian woman, Helena Blavatsky. She was living in New York and displayed strong psychic talents as well as having much to say about the universe in general and psychic phenomena in particular. The objectives of the Theosophical Society include the study of all religions and philosophies. Some branches have chosen to adhere only to Blavatsky's teachings, while others pursue a wide field of research as Blavatsky herself recommended.

Theosophy teaches that a person is a pure spirit that is reincarnated in life after life. Both his mind and his emotions are not part of the spirit, but are renewed with a personality that develops with each new incarnation. A person is thus said to have a "higher self" (the immortal spirit) and a "lower self" (mind, body and emotions) which is the temporary abode of the spirit during any lifetime. Theosophists claim that there are two distinct types of psychic ability: one belonging to the lower self, the other to the higher self.

Ordinary ESP is said to be part of the lower self. It is therefore weak, imperfect and unreliable and to meddle with it is said to be not only a waste of time but even dangerous in certain circumstances. For an imperfect human being to develop his psychic power is said to be like giving an atomic bomb to a child for a plaything. It is far better, according to the Theosophists, to develop the spiritual nature and forget about psychic ability. All highly evolved spiritual beings are said to possess spiritual powers far beyond anything an ordinary person can do. Theosophists class these as the "higher psychic" abilities to distinguish them from the "lower psychic" ones we all possess to a limited degree. Many Theosophists tend to look down on people who are interested in psychic phenomena, although many liberal branches of the Society have published books on psychical research. The world has also known some fine Theosophical clairvoyants. Charles Leadbeater and Geoffrey Hodgson are Theosophists who have written books about their own psychic experiences. It is also said by the Theosophists that if a person sets out to perfect himself through meditation and yogic techniques, he will initially lose any psychic talent he has. But if he succeeds in reaching his spiritual goals, he will eventually attain full spiritual powers much greater than the ones he gave up.

Now these theories all sound convincing, but some serious questions can be asked about their validity. It is known that ESP is usually irregular and unreliable and this would fit with the theory that it is therefore a product of our "lower self". However, no-one has suggested that to develop your physical muscles is dangerous and muscles are certainly as "low" as you can go on the spiritual scale. As long as we have an ordinary life to lead, there can be no harm in using the ordinary potential we have brought into this lifetime. Certainly there are people who have misused their talents, but the fault lies in the person, not in the talent. Frankly, I believe that the claim that ESP is of no importance sounds like a case of sour grapes since people who do have ESP are never the ones who put forth this view.

The theory that highly evolved beings possess complete control of their psychic powers also sounds reasonable but there is little evidence that it is true. There has never yet been a person who was universally agreed to be spiritually evolved, at least not until several centuries after the person had died. Curiously, tales of the supernatural abilities of the saints also seem to develop years after their deaths, along with the conviction that they were genuinely saintly. Blavatsky talked of spiritually advanced men living in Tibet who had miraculous powers, but these mahatmas seem unwilling to reveal themselves to anyone except devout Theosophists. Blavatsky herself possessed considerable psychic ability (along with a bag of tricks similar to the shamans among whom she had travelled in Mongolia and Central Asia). She also possessed a thoroughly earthy personality with no visible saintly qualities. In short, the theory that the way to real psychic power is through spiritual development seems to be just that, a theory. Until there is a person who can not only walk through walls but also convince everybody of his or her *bona fide* spiritual status, the Theosophical theory must remain unproven. It is also noticeable that just as genuinely psychic people seldom go in for the "lower psychic" and "higher psychic" theory, so too they are not conspicuously more saintly than anybody else. At least two of the most psychic people I have ever met could be positively unpleasant in their dealings with those around them.

Around the time that the Theosophical Society was founded, a number of scientists began to study the whole field of psychic phenomena. At first their work was referred to as "psychical research" but today it is more generally known as "parapsychology". The early psychic researchers investigated Spiritualism which, at that time, claimed to be producing an enormous variety of supernatural goings-on. Almost unanimously, the researchers concluded that these were not due to the action of spirits but rather to the minds of the Spiritualists who attended the seances. A good deal of fraud was also uncovered and over the next three decades many of the phenomena died out as medium after medium was exposed in trickery. While some scientists, notably the psychical researcher Sir Oliver Lodge, believed that the spirit really does survive death and may communicate with the living, most agreed that many Spiritualist phenomena were the result of the abilities of the living people, not dead ones.

Modern-day parapsychologists tend to concentrate upon testing people for ESP in laboratory experiments rather than investigating seances. Since the pioneering work of the researcher Dr J. B. Rhine, there has been an enormous volume of research based upon card-guessing experiments in which volunteers make thousands of guesses in the hope of scoring more than is likely through chance and thus proving that ESP is at work.

What sort of theories and discoveries has parapsychology made? One of the first discoveries was that a card-guessing experiment that works well once will probably *not* work well the next time. This has produced thousands of experiments which are successful only on the first attempt. The only indisputable conclusions (apart from the basic finding that ESP definitely exists) are as follows:

1. Most people who score above chance in such experiments tend to do less well as they go on, usually finishing with only average results — their ability to use ESP dies out. This is known as the "decline effect" and many people have put forth suggestions on how to avoid it. The most obvious fact here is that card-guessing actually discourages ESP! Yet many parapsychologists insist on continuing with these experiments.

2. ESP is totally unaffected by physical restrictions such as distance, electrical interference, lead sheeting, etcetera. This is particularly important because it disproves the theory that ESP is like a radio wave, a theory that Russian scientists postulated early this century.

3. Some people score above average in experiments and some score below average. Since to score poorly when guessing thousands of times is just as difficult as to score well, it follows that someone who scores below average may be using ESP in the same way as someone who scores above average. (In a small number of guesses, say a dozen, it is easy to score above or below average. But when a greater number of tests are made, it is impossible to score either low or high unless something other than chance is at work. Chance will always give you an average result.) If you take a group of people who do not believe in ESP and another group who do believe in it, you are more likely to get below-average scores in the doubting group and above-average ones in the believing group. (Of course if none of them has any ESP at all, they will all score about average despite their beliefs.) This is one of the very few card-guessing experiments that usually works and has been dubbed the "sheep-and-goats effect". It shows that while your attitude may not influence whether you have ESP, it probably does influence how that ESP will operate.

The original objective of Rhine and his co-workers was to provide a large body of evidence that ESP does exist and then to investigate how it works. The first part of that objective has been achieved, so there seems little point in continuing it. If there is one thing that parapsychology has proved it is that laboratory guessing-games are a prime way to discourage ESP and a useless way to develop it. Unfortunately many parapsychologists have failed to notice this. In 1979 Charles Tart, one of America's most famous parapsychologists, published a book entitled, *Learning to Use ESP*. His theory is that if you reward a person as soon as he scores a correct guess, he will learn to make more correct guesses. Thus you will have developed his ESP. Charles Tart constructed some ingenious ways of arranging his tests, and published results showing that some subjects had achieved significantly higher scores than average. It remains to be seen whether anyone else can manage to repeat these experiments. While we can commend Tart for his efforts, it seems that none of his subjects has become psychic in the way that a good Spiritualist, clairvoyant, fortune-teller, witchdoctor or local gypsy teacup-reader is psychic. While it is pleasing to score well in card-guessing, it is of no earthly use for anything else.

You will notice that in Chapter One I listed all the things that this book can teach you to do. You will also notice that nowhere have I included anything about card-guessing. This is probably the most sterile technique of all and is not relevant to real psychic development. A modern suggestion that has grown out of the negative findings of laboratory ESP work is that all human beings have evolved the ability to emit a negative kind of psychic power which blocks the telepathic ability of everyone else. There are certain moths that radiate a high-pitched sound that interferes with the sonar system used by bats who prey on moths. If human beings unconsciously do the same thing with ESP, it would explain why ESP is so irregular and why, the moment ESP appears in an experiment, it starts to fade out so that the experiment cannot be repeated.

Such a theory is rather like postulating that there is an invisible pink elephant behind your chair. You cannot disprove it because the theory holds that you cannot see or detect the thing you have postulated. Such a theory is not worth considering because you cannot prove it one way or the other. A more obvious answer is that laboratory guessing-experiments discourage the operation of ESP. My own theory is that any sort of concentrated mental effort blocks out ESP and therefore laboratory experiments, by their very nature, encourage the rational parts of the mind and discourage the prerational psychic abilities.

Throughout history, there have been psychic people. Almost all religious and occult groups can point to one or more of their members who show strong psychic powers. But how many of them can claim that their entire group developed such powers? In most cases the psychic person started out with an obvious ESP talent and then merely employed or trained the ability under the auspices of the group to which he or she belonged. There are few cases of strongly psychic people who did not have some sort of ability right from childhood.

To be of general use a method of psychic development must be applicable to anyone, regardless of their natural talent. If my theory of ESP as set out in this chapter is correct, such a method also must have the following qualities:

1. It must be interesting and enjoyable to provide the incentive to persevere.
2. It must block out the reasoning part of the mind in order to let the ESP operate.
3. It must encourage the use of ESP, not merely permit it to function.
4. It must permit the person to maintain an intelligent discrimination and a level of commonsense so that imagination and self-delusion do not hold sway.

Perhaps this sounds like a great deal to be achieved through one method — yet it can certainly be done. My theory was developed after having stumbled across such a method and, in the next chapter, I will tell you exactly how to do it yourself.

Chapter Three
THE ONLY SURE-FIRE METHOD
FOR BECOMING PSYCHIC

If you are a person who drinks coffee rather than tea, prepare for a change because the humble teacup is your gateway to the path of psychic development. Tasseomancy, or teacup-reading, is the ideal way to stimulate whatever latent ESP you may possess.

Have you ever wondered how teacup-reading works or even whether it works at all? There are books which purport to teach this. They contain lists of symbols that you must memorise in order to hunt them out from among the tea-leaves. A cat is said to mean good luck, a bird symbolises news coming, and so forth. According to these books a would-be prophet need only memorise a few hundred meanings and, *voilà*, instant fortune-telling. Unfortunately this is not the way good teacup-reading works. Let me tell you the real secret of the cups and how it can be used for your own psychic development.

At one time I lived in a town where gypsy tearooms flourished. For 90 cents the proprietress served a small plate of toast or buns and a pot of tea which you dutifully consumed before getting on with the real business: having your fortune told. The customer would upend the empty teacup, then carefully carry it to where the sibyl sat enthroned behind a card table. She would earnestly survey the tea-leaves in the cup, pause for a moment of ominous silence, then launch into 10 minutes of commentary on the next week or so in your life.

I liked the tearooms and often called in whenever a good reader was at work. They were cosy and delightfully informal, filled with old ladies and clusters of housewives, with an occasional table of giggling schoolgirls excited by this brush with the occult. Male faces were rare, though sometimes a man would slip in and perch awkwardly at the corner of a table before carrying his cup over to the seer as eagerly as any of the women. Many of the customers were regulars and I could be sure of seeing a familiar face almost every time I called in.

The tearooms employed a different reader for every day of the week. Many of them worked a regular run of tearooms to ensure a full week's work. It was easy to tell when a good reader was in session as there would inevitably be a crowd waiting outside the door long before opening time. One or two readers could barely attract any customers: people would peer in at them and then quickly turn away.

One Friday in 1970 I stopped by a favourite tearoom. The owner, who knew me well, stopped to chat. "I'm in a bit of a jam, Andrew," she told me. "My reader for tomorrow can't make it, and it's now too late to get a fill-in. You know a lot about this sort of thing. Could you take her place? It's Saturday, only a half-day's work."

I was nonplussed. I had never read a teacup in my life, nor had I ever considered doing so. However, I knew how the readers worked. They spent 10 minutes with each customer, giving a string of small, inconsequential predictions about the week ahead. Their readings consisted largely of such common events as visits, letters, purchases and minor domestic scenes. Nobody expected them to solve major problems or predict earth-shattering events. I made up my mind quickly. "Sure," I told her, "I may not be very good, but I'll be happy to help you out."

On leaving the tearoom I went into a nearby bookstore and bought a book on reading tea-leaves. On the way home I glanced through and was dismayed to discover 120 pages of symbols listed alphabetically. I learned that an axe in the cup was a sure sign of a separation to come, while a zebra heralded the arrival of news from Africa. Somehow, I did not foresee finding many zebras in the cups on Saturday.

It all looked rather overwhelming. I decided I had better play the thing by ear rather than memorise 120 pages. Surely I could improvise for a few hours, using my own imagination. In the meantime two friends had arrived at my place for a visit. I decided to brew up a pot of tea for them. When we had all ceremoniously turned our cups over, I picked up one and inspected its clustered leaves.

"Well, there's a dog," I ventured. "I guess it must be a lost dog."

"Why, yes. There was a lost dog nosing in our yard this morning," said my friend Louise. Her husband, Martin, murmured agreement. I was mildly surprised.

"There seems to be a broken shape here. You'd better beware of breaking something, eh?" I went on. Louise nodded. Altogether I made about a dozen comments by observing the leaves and letting my imagination have free play about the possible meaning. Besides my hit with the lost dog, one other comment seemed relevant. It was my last attempt, made after a string of apparent failures. I saw a leaf floating in a drop of moisture and said, "That looks like something being washed down the sink".

"That's right!" said Louise. "I lost a coin down the sink yesterday. I was quite annoyed by it." This was a striking coincidence, and it gave me the confidence to inspect Martin's cup in the same way.

On Saturday morning I made my way to the tearoom. Before long a steady stream of women were bringing me their teacups. I made a few jokes, told them all that the future looked rosy and said whatever came into my head based on the chance patterns of tea-leaves. I overheard two of the ladies talking. "He's good," whispered one of them. My ego was definitely inflated. When we closed at 1 p.m. the proprietress paid me $3.30 for my work: 30 readings at 11 cents each. I went home highly amused by the whole episode.

The following week, Louise said to me, "You know how you warned me about something breaking? Well, I broke a saucer on Monday. And on Tuesday Martin had to halt the car suddenly when a kid ran across the road, just as you had told him." I was intrigued to hear this.

Over the next few weeks, whenever someone offered me tea I asked to read their teacup in return. The results were interesting. In each reading there were always one or two items applying to the person's immediate past or present circumstances. There were also remarks like, "That sounds right" or, "That makes sense" from the client, confirming that what I had said seemed relevant. I put it all down to coincidence, but was nonetheless fascinated.

Six weeks later I was sitting with a female acquaintance who mentioned her interest in psychic things. I told her all about my teacups. She insisted that it was not coincidence but rather ESP at work. This I strongly denied. "Oh yes it is," she countered. "You really don't need a teacup to do it though. That's just a crutch. You can pick things up without mucking about with tea-leaves."

To prove her wrong, I volunteered to attempt psychometrising a ring she wore. Psychometrising is the method of perceiving psychically impressions about a person, while holding an object belonging to that person in order to start the flow of information. I was confident that nothing would come of this. She handed the ring over, and I closed my eyes and waited to see what would happen. Of course, nothing did. And then, into the blankness of my mind, an idea floated — an impression of a small glass bell. So I told her, "I can see a small glass bell".

"That's right!" she replied. "At night, I take off all my rings and keep them on the neck of a glass bell on my dressing-table. You see, you can do it after all." To say I was flabbergasted would be an understatement.

So that is how it all started. I wondered afterwards whether she might have made it up in order to encourage me. But much later I visited her home and saw the bell on the dresser, exactly as she had said. You have heard enough of my personal experiences. It is time to go on to some specific instructions for your own development. Here is the programme that I originally set up for my friends Martin and Louise and which you can easily adapt to your own circumstances.

Martin, Louise, a girlfriend and myself set up our own psychic research club, meeting once a week for experiments. For a year or more we worked with a ouija and with zener cards. (Zener cards are the standard cards bearing five symbols, which are used for testing ESP.) Then we turned our attention towards teacup-reading. At the end of every meeting, each of us would attempt readings for the others. A written list was made of every comment. A tick mark was placed beside anything that applied to the previous week of the person's life. The following week the list was checked once more and a further mark placed beside anything that had occurred in the meantime. We kept a careful record of our successes and failures and discovered that our marks improved as the weeks progressed.

On the first attempt Martin scored two successes out of 12 tries. By the fourth week he was scoring five out of 10. On the eighth week we noted that four of the 11 things that Martin had named had been true at the time and the other seven occurred during the week. He was 100 per cent accurate on both postcognitive and precognitive impressions! Furthermore he found that he could usually tell whether an impression applied to the past or the future.

All four of us were regularly scoring at least 50 per cent accuracy, all with a mixture of past and future items. None of the things we picked up proved to be of great importance, but there could be no doubt that we were developing genuine ESP. This is exactly the sort of programme I suggest you take up. Begin by reading for acquaintances — tell them it is just for fun, and that they are not to expect too much. After your first couple of attempts keep a record of all your impressions in a notebook. Be sure to check back each week in case any of them were predictions. It is absolutely vital that a notebook be kept — tasseomancy can only succeed as a method of psychic development if it is accompanied by accurate record-keeping. The reason for this will become clear later.

When you look into a teacup use your imagination to pick out patterns in the leaves. Do not hunt for stylised items like birds, animals or the letters of the alphabet. Let your fancy roam. No matter how strange or how ordinary the leaf patterns seem, if they resemble something, say so. Always say the first thing that occurs to you — never ponder over a shape or try to puzzle it out. Do not worry about whether what you see is relevant to the person nor whether it seems probable or improbable. The objective is to give your first, instinctive impressions about the tea-leaf shapes, not to study and evaluate them.

Imagination can help you do more than just identify the shapes. It will often give a little extra. Remember when I saw a dog and added, "I guess it must be a lost dog"? There was no particular reason why I said that, except that it simply occurred to me. Try to avoid symbolism. If you see a pot, call it a pot. Do not take it as a symbol for something else. Take no notice of the symbolic interpretations you will find in books. They have no place in what you are doing here.

Another common idea to disregard is that the position of a shape in the cup indicates how far into the future it will occur. Some theories maintain that the higher up a pattern lies, the closer to the present time it is. Such a system restricts the free flow of your imagination. The important thing is to have no restrictions at all. After a while you will find that you can guess an approximate date without using any system at all. If you get an impression of time, do not hesitate to say so. You will find that if you want to get such impressions, they will start to form.

Just as impressions of time will often occur if you seek them, so, too, making a conscious effort to score successes will help. At first, without experience, you will have no control over successes or failures. As you progress you will find that your own desire and intent will help you to succeed and improve. Teacup-reading is not a very impressive psychic feat, but it is an ideal way to get started. For a non-psychic person exercising the imagination on random tea-leaves will stimulate any latent psychic ability that may be there. Can you see why?

By using your imagination you are turning off the rational part of your mind. If you were to work to a set of rules it would require a conscious, rational effort. By working without rules, but nevertheless with a desire to find patterns, you are resting the rational mind and letting the irrational take over. Of course you may get a lot of pure imagination, but you also get a proportion of psychic "hits". Since it is the psychic element you want, your own desire will ensure that you get more of it. The more you practise, the more you get, as long as you keep your mind relaxed, imaginative and free.

This is where the record-keeping comes in. By keeping a tally of your successes and failures, you can evaluate exactly how much imagination and how much ESP you are getting. As long as you keep records, imagination will never run away with you and there is no danger of turning into a fraud. But just as surely, if you fail to keep records there will never be an improvement in your work. This is the "believing–doubting tightrope" we talked about — you must balance your belief in what you are doing with the constant checking of records.

There are some other factors that help the system work. The

most important of these is the light-hearted atmosphere which teacup-reading invariably generates. To sit around drinking tea is a pleasant social activity, while a little fortune-telling appeals to everyone. Teacup-reading is fun. The reader is in a relaxed, positive frame of mind while also possessing the incentive to succeed. He or she has turned off the rational part of the mind but maintains the safeguard of record-keeping. Everything combines to make this a perfect set-up.

Your successes with teacup-reading will probably never amount to anything startling, but you will certainly find that your amateur readings are popular. You may find teacups being thrust into your hands wherever you go. Undoubtedly you will be drinking more tea from now on than you ever did before.

Let us suppose that you have now been practising tasseomancy for a month, having reached the point of invariably scoring successes when you read a cup. It is now time to move on. Pick an acquaintance (not a close friend) and ask if you can try some psychometry. Explain that you are experimenting. Ask the person to rate you on whatever success you achieve. Request that they hand you a ring or watch or any personal item. Hold it in your hand and relax your mind, just as you learned to do when reading teacups. See what you can pick up.

This is one of the most important "jumps" you will ever make in your psychic development. Up to now you have had something to help you; now you must simply open yourself to impressions. If you are anything like me, you will feel a moment of panic when you first try it. But without doubt some sort of mental picture or impression will float into your mind and you must immediately describe it. With any luck it will be something relevant. If not, try again and keep going until you have offered half a dozen comments. In all probability one or two statements will be correct and you will know that your training through teacup-reading was not in vain. Your mind is now accustomed to freeing your ESP whenever you want it to.

Avoid generalisations when practising your ESP. There is a temptation to fall back on statements like: "You have been tired", "There has been a health problem", "You seem tense, anxious, overworked, concerned, to be making plans", etcetera. Instead go for specifics: objects, incidents, statements that are definitely either right or wrong. Even if the person *is* tired, overworked, tense or what-have-you, it is far clearer and better to tell him or her, "You have just been to the dentist", or "You bought a new television set". It may not matter very much to the client, but it is a specific psychic impression which, unlike generalisations, cannot be accounted for otherwise.

You should also try to obtain facts about the present rather than predictions for the future. At this stage it is not easy to differentiate between them when you pick them up. But obviously current facts can be confirmed more readily than things that still lie in the future. If you have succeeded with teacups, your first attempt at psychometry should prove successful. If it does not, do not give up. Try again with someone else, perhaps two or three others. Sooner or later you will succeed. The chances are high that you will do so right from the start.

There is a reason why your first attempts should be made with people you do not know well. All psychics find that it is easier to read for strangers than for close friends. This is because your mind is already filled with impressions and ideas about the people you know. When you are learning it is wise to work entirely with people about whom you know little or nothing. Later, when you are more experienced, you may try the more difficult task of reading for friends.

This rule does *not* apply with tasseomancy because the tea-leaves give you a definite medium to work with. In psychometry there is only your mind and if your mind already knows the person, you are bound to have difficulty. However, once you have developed some skill with psychometry you should leave the tea-cups alone. The reason for this is that the tea-leaves actually restrict the flow of ESP, even though they are the perfect means of stimulating it at the beginning. Your imagination uses the leaves to find patterns and images, but this limits you to what you can find in those patterns. As long as you are thus limited, your ESP cannot develop further. Tasseomancy is an excellent beginning, but you must use other methods too in order to progress. This does not mean you must never read another teacup. Even today I have friends who thrust teacups into my hand with the cry, "Quick! Tell me something good that's going to happen!". I never turn them down. But I always tell them that it is just for fun and not to be taken too seriously.

Several books have been written on psychometry and, unlike the volumes on teacup-reading, there is no harm in going through some of these. However, there is one idea often put forward by psychometrists that needs to be squashed from the start. This is the idea that objects somehow carry a psychic record of what has happened to them, which the psychometrist then reads like a book. This view shows psychometry as being akin to playing a record. While it is true that this can happen, it is only part of the truth and is therefore misleading. There is plenty of evidence that psychometrists can tell where an object has been and what has happened to its owner. There are also cases where the psychometrist gets all sorts of additional information. But this information cannot be regarded as a psychic record somehow imbedded in the object. There are also cases where the psychometrist has had excellent results while working with the wrong object; that is, while reading for one person with another person's object. Geoffrey Hodgson, the New Zealand clairvoyant, once psychometrised two fossilised bones and perfectly described the animals from which they came . . . except each description actually applied to the other fossil! Thus it appears that the object is more a focal point than a recording. We could liken it to a radio set tuned to a certain station rather than to a record being played.

Nevertheless, there are certain rules that help. One is that heavy or dense articles work better than light ones. Metal or glass are superior to cloth or paper and plastic is seldom any good at all. Items much used by their owners seem to work better than those touched only occasionally. Old articles are more useful to the psychometrist than new ones. A pair of spectacles is often an ideal object to work with since it is made of relatively dense materials and is in constant use. Watches are also good, but rings are often too small and are seldom easy to work with.

Some psychometrists find they get better results when holding an item to their forehead or neck. This is a matter for personal experimentation. I am inclined to think that it depends on your own expectations or beliefs — if you think that holding it to your elbow will help, then perhaps it will. In my own experiments I have occasionally worked with people who have no object to offer. With them I have had good results by getting them to sign their name on a piece of paper and then psychometrising the signature. Everyone who works with psychometry develops their own approach and tends to become better as they grow more familiar with the procedure. Using ESP reminds me of learning to ride a bicycle. At first it seems impossible. Then one day you get the hang of it and, before long, it seems as easy as walking.

Like learning to ride a bicycle, however, practice is essential. As stated in Chapter One, developing your ESP does take work; but it is work that pays off. Along with practice, you must maintain a desire to improve. This is very important. As long as you are trying to do better, you will. Never be satisfied with your current standards: strive for higher ones. You may ask, "But how *do* I improve?" The only answer to this is to try. Martin found that he could date events in the tea-leaves merely by trying to do so. You will find that as long as you want to improve, and honestly try, you will succeed. Once your psychic ability has opened up your own desire and intent will do the trick. Before you have opened the door no amount of ambition or effort will help you to become psychic. Once you have developed the knack of picking up impressions your own determination will work wonders.

This brings us back to the "believing–doubting tightrope" again. You must always temper your desire for success by an honest evaluation of exactly what you get right and what you get wrong. There will always be a proportion of mistakes, though this will lessen as you progress. It is essential that you notice and remember them in order not to be carried away. While you are still training, never undertake a reading if the results cannot be verified. I once knew a psychic who told me she often sat in a bus silently reading other passengers. No wonder her psychic ability started to deteriorate! She had no way of knowing if her impressions were right, and merely assumed that they must be. Her psychic readings soon became filled with all sorts of purely imaginative impressions.

I would also advise you never to pick up an object and try to psychometrise its history unless there is some way of checking that your impressions are correct. When you are an experienced psychic you may risk doing such a thing. Do not attempt it while you are still learning. Even when you are experienced such experiments should only be tried rarely and should fit in between other readings which can readily be checked. In such cases you should make a special note of the fact that your impressions cannot be proved. Never assume that they are bound to be correct.

In the same way, when reading for a person try to pick up plenty of facts about the present along with predictions for the future. Here are some anecdotes to further illustrate some aspects of psychometry.

I once visited a small country museum with a group of friends. The town was little more than a village and the museum was filled with an eclectic array of odds and ends donated by the local people. One of the women in our party wandered into a side room. When she came out she announced that there was something very creepy about it. We went to investigate and we all concluded that there was indeed an unpleasant feeling about the room. I prowled around, checking out every object in the place and decided that the feeling was concentrated in an old barber's chair which stood in one corner. On touching it I picked up the immediate impression of a man in pain, suffering from a terrible cancer of the face.

We went back and spoke to the manager of the museum, a taciturn fellow who told us that he had no knowledge of the barber's chair. However, when I remarked on the impression I had picked up, he stared at me in wonder. "Now why would you say that?" he demanded slowly. "As a matter of fact, that chair was donated by a man who died of cancer." Obviously, in this case, the painful illness which afflicted the owner of the chair had impressed itself so strongly onto the chair that the impression could be felt by anyone entering the room. No doubt the fact that the chair was a massive heavy object helped.

The second case concerns a friend who bought a curious sheet of thick curved glass which he used as a small table for his telephone. One day when I was visiting his home he invited me to tell him anything about its history. On touching the glass I received the impression of a man shaving. My friend laughed and congratulated me. That very morning he had been shaving when the phone rang. On running out to answer it he had placed his electric razor on the glass — the razor had set up a vibration which amused him and he had then run the razor backward and forward for the effect. Now the point of the story is that my mental picture had been of a man shaving with a straight-edged razor. I was therefore strikingly right in what I said, but wrong in the way I had envisioned it. My mental picture was no doubt drawn from some subconscious memory of a picture in a book, which popped into my consciousness to accompany the impression picked up.

Speaking of the way one's own mind tends to shape the way one perceives what is psychically tuned into, I would mention that invariably, when I have psychically described a building and subsequently seen that building, I have found my description was only a particular point of view. That is to say, the description matched the building as seen from only one direction, rather than being an overall view.

The essential mechanism used in psychometry is that of stilling the flow of thoughts while holding onto an object, with the intention of letting through psychic impressions. When you are familiar with this procedure, you will realise that holding an object is not really necessary. It is perfectly possible to read for a person merely by sitting or standing near him or her and stilling your mind in the same way. In theory it is also possible to do this at a distance, without being able to see the person. Certainly there are times when this has indeed been done. However, I must admit that in practice it is easier to work for a person who is present and, best of all, to have a good object to psychometrise. I am inclined to think that this is simply a psychological effect, since even the most confident psychic likes to have something solid on which to focus. Perhaps there will come a time when we can effortlessly obtain psychic impressions of anyone or anything in the world. But I certainly have not gone that far . . . yet!

One useful way to sharpen your ESP is with what I call "psychic game-playing". It is not a method for development, but it is an effective way to practise once your ESP is working. To begin, whenever a letter arrives in the mail, hold it for a moment before opening and try to guess the contents. Often you will pick up an impression. If you do this regularly you must keep a record of your results. Another good game is to make a weekly or monthly effort to sense something about your own future. Spend five minutes or so writing down anything that comes into your head; check the results at the end of the week or month. In your everyday life there will be many opportunities to test your powers. If you are going shopping, pause for a moment to sense if there is a particular shop you should go to or a specific bargain waiting for you. When driving, test your sense of where the possibility of a parking space may be or the best route for avoiding traffic snarls.

When you are introduced to new people, try to get an impression of them. Be sure to check up afterwards to see if you are correct. Telephones are a fruitful source of psychic impressions. Many ordinary people have had the experience of hearing the phone ring and guessing correctly who was on the other end. If you try to do this yourself you will often be able to name the caller. Ever since the telephone came into common use observant people have noticed it has a curious link with ESP. A writer in the *Occult Review* nearly 50 years ago proposed a new word, "phonevoyance", to describe clairvoyance on the telephone as so many people had experienced it. I have met at least three psychics who could describe what the person at the other end of the line was wearing or doing. Why not see if you can do this too? You will find that you can often "read" successfully for someone in another town merely by talking to him or her on the phone.

Use your imagination to see how many ways you can practise ESP around your home or at work. If you regard it as a game and treat it as such, you will be amazed at the results. I am inclined to think that a dozen different games, each played only once or twice a week, will give you better results than the same game played over and over. There are two games that I like to play myself. One is giving psychic impressions at parties — I often find that in a social gathering where everyone is having fun, particularly if the food and wine are flowing freely, impressions about the lives of the party-goers come bursting into my mind. Because I do not do any professional psychic readings, I do not find myself often reading for other people. But at parties, or even when one or two folks get together for a discussion, I commonly sense things so strongly that I am almost impelled to talk about them.

The other psychic game is a special one. Some years ago I met a woman with whom I experienced a type of telepathy. Often I would be about to say something when she would say it first. Or I would speak and it would turn out that this was what she had been thinking. Obviously this was a case of two minds being closely attuned so that we picked up each other's thoughts without realising it. We developed a simple game which increased the frequency of these telepathic flashes. Whenever one occurred the person who had not spoken first would call out, "Strike!" to verify that they had been thinking of the same thing. When we first adopted this habit we were tuning into each other about once a day. Before very long we were calling "Strike!" about once an hour.

Our practice of calling out drew attention to the telepathic flashes and, by doing this, we caused them to become more and more frequent. Since then I have done the same thing with two other people and obtained the same results. I have also met people who tell me they have telepathic flashes with one of their friends, and I have recommended the "Strike" game to them with good results.

In Chapter One, I mentioned finding lost objects. This is another useful way to employ your ESP. There is no particular method involved: simply pause, clear your mind in the usual way, and an impression of where the object is will pop into your mind. Sometimes it can help to do it in two stages: start by finding the approximate area where the object is located and then make a second attempt to find the exact position. I must admit that the process sometimes requires two or three tries and that it sometimes fails completely. However, it works more often than not, sometimes on the first attempt, usually on a second or third. Unfortunately it is almost impossible to do this for yourself. You can find things for other people, but if *you* lose something, you had better call in another psychic. The problem here is that ESP does not work well if your mind is already cluttered with facts and ideas, which is the case when the lost object is your own. Like all uses of ESP, locating lost objects may go astray though your psychic impressions are correct. I was once approached by a friend who had lost two kittens. Anne had been caring for a stray cat that had given birth in her back garden. Like all cats, this one took to carrying its children around from one hiding place to another. One day it was killed by a car shortly after secreting the kittens in a new place.

Anne came to me for help. We drove to her house where I "tuned in'' and decided that the kittens were under a house (Queensland homes are built on stumps above the ground). They were near an old green car and beside a pile of used tyres. I nominated the direction I thought was correct and we set off. For an hour we prowled along the road, trying to inspect every house along the way. Nowhere could we find the lost kittens. Eventually, returning home in despair, Anne gave a cry and darted into the grounds of a house. She had seen the flash of a tail and, sure enough, under the house were our lost animals. They were playing in a pile of tyres beside an old green car which had been propped up on bricks. So my psychic impression had been correct but had not helped find the kittens. It was Anne's sharp eyes which found them and my ESP had counted for little, only pointing out the direction in which to walk.

Tasseomancy and psychometry, as well as the psychic games, practised as I have directed will bring out your ESP in the shortest possible time. Why spend years studying? Why pay large sums of money for psychic courses when in a few short weeks you can be as psychic as the most professional readers? And yet, though I have tested this system on several people and know that it works, I doubt that many of my readers will carry it through. There seem to be certain personality features that incline some people to do these things, while others, capable of doing just as well, never get around to it.

The ideal psychic reader is keen and enthusiastic. He or she wants to succeed; and enjoys trying. Nine times out of 10 the person has a cheerful, optimistic nature. He or she wants to use ESP, not because it will bring riches or fame, but because it is a fun thing to do. He or she usually likes being the centre of attention and is not afraid of making a few mistakes along the way. So what do you do if this does not sound anything like you? My advice is to try anyway. You cannot completely change your nature, but you can make an effort to summon up a bit of enthusiasm even if you are naturally dour. Of all I have just said, enjoyment is perhaps the key word. If you cannot get some fun out of what you are doing, you will probably never go far, even if your latent talent is great.

In this chapter, you have learned about several psychic techniques. If you apply them as I have directed, you will soon be well on the way to becoming a successful psychic reader. In the next few chapters, we will look at some more ways in which this ability can be directed and applied.

Chapter Four

THE SPIRIT WORLD —
DOS AND DON'TS
OF SPIRITUALISM

You cannot venture far into psychical investigation without encountering Spiritualism. Whatever form your research takes sooner or later it will lead to the Spiritualists, so it is useful to know what to expect right from the start. In the preceding chapters I have made several critical comments about Spiritualism. Nevertheless, I myself am a Spiritualist; I definitely believe in life after death. I also believe that it is possible to make contact with the spirit world. However, many of the Spiritualist practices actually hinder the development of ESP. It is also true that some displays that pass as spirit communication are in fact no such thing. You need a good deal of discrimination to sort the wheat from the chaff.

Throughout history there have always been cases of apparent contact with spirits. However, it was not until 1848 that the modern religious movement known as Spiritualism began in the small American town of Hydesville, New York. It soon spread around the world. From simple beginnings a variety of psychic phenomena rapidly became incorporated into the movement. All sorts of amazing things were said to occur: levitation, the sudden appearance or disappearance of solid objects and the materialisation of spirit bodies are just a few examples. Spiritualist mediums began to claim supernatural powers, such as immunity to fire, elongation of the body and X-ray vision. These phenomena were supposed to accompany the true core of Spiritualism, that is, communication with the spirits of the dead.

This communication was supposedly accomplished by various means. The main ones used today are known as "automatic phenomena". One method is table-rapping, in which a table bounces up and down under the hands of a group of people so that the knocking on the floor spells out spirit messages. A much more advanced method is to place a glass on a board inscribed with letters of the alphabet (known as a ouija board). When several people put their fingers on the glass it moves around the board to spell out sentences. Yet another variation is to construct a small board on wheels with a pencil attached. When touched, the board rolls around and the pencil forms writing. The final development in this genre is for the medium to hold a pencil in his or her hand and, without conscious awareness, write out spirit messages.

The second type of spirit communication uses trance. A medium passes into a trance state while spirits supposedly take over the body. He or she may speak in different voices or the face may change shape and appearance. The medium might speak in languages he or she does not know or paint or draw in a manner not normally possible. It is in these trance states that phenomena such as levitation are said to occur.

Thirdly, a Spiritualist may learn to see or hear spirits clairvoyantly. Strictly speaking, seeing is "clairvoyance" while hearing is known as "clairaudience". Spiritualist clairvoyants pass on messages from the spirits they perceive.

The fourth class of spirit contact is that created by the spirits themselves. Disembodied voices may be heard in the air. Knocks or blows can sound on the floor or ceiling with no visible cause. Written messages might appear spontaneously on a piece of paper or a slate. Spiritualists believe that the spirits draw energy from people in the room in order to create these manifestations. On rare occasions spirits may materialise into a solid visible form which dematerialises again at the end of the seance.

Of course all these phenomena can be imitated by tricks and, without doubt, this has happened countless times. Some scientists doubt whether materialisation or levitations have ever genuinely occurred, while others believe that they have. In this chapter only those phenomena that can be classed as extrasensory perception will be dealt with. We are not concerned with the whole range of supernatural happenings, merely those relevant to the development of your own psychic awareness.

The first thing to do when investigating Spiritualism is to visit a Spiritualist church — most cities have several, but smaller towns may not possess one. The religion-notices page of your local newspaper will tell you. Since Spiritualist churches seldom insist on any point of theology or doctrine, you are welcome to visit them whatever your own religious beliefs or persuasion. A typical service lasts between one and two hours. It will consist of assorted prayers and hymns, followed by a lecture and a display of clairvoyance. It is the latter that distinguishes a Spiritualist service from any other. For half an hour or more a clairvoyant stands up and gives messages to people in the congregation. Sometimes everyone receives a message, other times only a few do. These messages are supposedly from the spirits of the dead or else psychic perceptions about your life made by the clairvoyant.

When Spiritualism first started the purpose of these public displays was to provide evidence of life after death. By describing the spirits of your deceased relatives or friends, and getting relevant messages from them, the Spiritualists sought to prove that life goes on after the death of the physical body.

Unfortunately many so-called clairvoyants are quite unable to do this. Their displays have degenerated into a string of generalisations or wild guesses which are far from impressive.

Many churches have found that people mainly attend the services in the hope of receiving a message. Accordingly, the clairvoyants aim to give a message to everyone in the congregation rather than concentrating on getting real evidence of life after death. This has led to demonstrations in which the clairvoyant races from person to person, saying a few words to everyone and providing no evidence of anything. The people who attend such services do not want to be convinced, they merely want a few moments of attention from the supposed clairvoyant. Strangers who wander into the church usually leave convinced that the Spiritualists are a lot of gullible fools; their conclusion is often justified.

My own early experiences with Spiritualism consisted of visiting the six churches in my hometown. I soon decided that half the mediums had no ESP at all, while the others showed varying degrees of ability. The best of them would sometimes score some dramatic successes, juxtaposed with plenty of errors. There were only two mediums who proved to be right more often than they were wrong. Invariably they covered their failures with a variety of techniques, designed to draw attention away from the inadequacies. I noticed that the majority of the people attending were uncomplicated, sincere folk who accepted most things without question.

One day an announcement appeared locally that a new Scottish medium would be demonstrating at one of the churches. He was Bill Rowan, today widely known in Australia and Great Britain where he tours extensively. On the appointed evening I wandered down to the church. It was a small place, built into what had once been a private house. Inside there was room for about 40 hard-backed chairs, most of them already occupied when I arrived. There was little in the way of decoration and the place felt stuffy from the tightly packed crowd. A platform stood at one end of the church where two men and the organist were seated. One of the men was the president of the church, a thick-set, muscular man who looked as if he could tackle a grizzly bear with no effort. The other was Bill Rowan.

At that time he was about 50. Bill was stockily built with a pleasant but unremarkable face which could easily be lost in a crowd. He could have been a butcher or baker and did not look like the sort of man to be in contact with the spirit world. When he spoke, a heavy Scottish burr broke the air. His vocabulary was excellent, while the overall use of language was both impressive and entertaining. I learned later that he spent years training himself to speak in public. When the time came for the demonstration, Bill spent a few minutes explaining how he worked. Then he launched into the messages.

"May I speak to the lady there, please? Can you hear my voice?"

"Yes," she replied.

"There's a woman standing beside you, in spirit, who tells me she is your sister. She passed over several years ago. Is that correct?"

"That's right," she replied.

"She says you used to have a photograph of her with you and your father, but that you've lost it."

"Yes, I left it behind in my last house after we moved."

"Well, she remembers it. She tells me that you had a brother, too, who's passed over, but he's not here now."

"That's right," the woman repeated.

"She's asking why you don't play the piano like you did when she was alive?"

"Because I don't have a piano any more." There was general laughter. Bill made one or two more comments, then moved on to someone else.

"You, sir, the gentleman in the dark suit. Can you hear my voice?"

"Yes, Bill, I hear you."

"There's a man here who says his name is John Middleton and that he worked with your father."

"That's right. My dad was a barber and John was his partner. My dad's dead too."

"Well, I haven't got your father, but Mr Middleton is here and wants to say hello. He was a tall man and walked with a limp."

And so it went. Bill continued from person to person and though some of his descriptions were not recognised, nearly everything he said proved to be relevant. The whole focus of Bill's work is upon contact with spirits. He makes little attempt to describe people's lives or to prophesy the future. Instead he concentrates on describing spirits and, having successfully done so, he goes on to relate whatever the spirit may want to communicate. Often these messages refer to incidents from the past, known both to the spirit and to the person with whom Bill is talking. Sometimes the spirits claim to be interested in the life of the person in question and will offer comments on their home, work or present circumstances.

Time after time I have seen Bill Rowan select a stranger from the congregation and launch into a detailed description of his or her deceased father, uncle or aunt which proves to be completely true. Usually the spirit has something to say, and if the person cares to reply there will soon be a conversation passing back and forth with Bill relaying the spirit's comments to the person concerned. Bill has often commented that his role is rather like that of a telephone. He is the means of communication between the living and the dead. In point of fact this is the origin of the word "medium". A medium is a means of communication just as air is the medium through which sound travels. Unfortunately very few Spiritualist mediums live up to the meaning of the word.

Bill Rowan readily admits that some of what he picks up comes from his own ESP. Unlike many Spiritualists Bill has a good understanding of ESP, the workings of the subconscious mind and the many criticisms that can be made of the occult and psychic fields. He likes to examine and investigate and without doubt this is one of the factors contributing to his success. Bill remarks that some of his information appears to come from the spirits, while some comes from his own perception. He also believes that he has spirit guides working with him who provide a third source of information. While working, it is not easy for him to discern how much of the information derives from each source. Since the object of the exercise is to prove survival after death, he always concentrates on that aspect of the demonstration as much as possible.

In the last 10 years I have seen many mediums at work and I would class Mr Rowan in the top 20 clairvoyants in the world. There are a few Spiritualists whose abilities surpass even Bill's, and there are probably several hundred who come close to his standard. There must be thousands who do not. Not long after I first saw Bill Rowan at work, the church announced that he was starting a series of development classes. I joined immediately and that is how I entered the Spiritualist movement. Under Bill's guidance and, later, through a lot of work on my own, I too developed the ability to perceive spirits. The process is not difficult. It is essentially just an extension of the basic ESP you learned about in Chapter Three. If you have carried out those exercises, you too can learn to become aware of the spirit world, thus gaining your own personal proof that life goes on after death.

Before we see how to do it, let us examine further how the Spiritualist movement is organised. Most Spiritualist churches are completely independent. Unlike those denominations in which all churches acknowledge the same headquarters, each Spiritualist church is a law unto itself. In some countries there are large Spiritualist organisations, but there may also be plenty of churches functioning outside the mainstream.

Some churches call themselves Christian Spiritualists. These employ readings from the Bible and acknowledge the leadership of Jesus. The other Spiritualists are not anti-Christian, but they do not regard Christianity to be superior to any of the other world religions. They consider Jesus as one of the many spiritual masters the world has known, rather than as the sole link between humankind and God. Many Spiritualists believe in re-incarnation. Their numbers seem to be increasing, though there are still many who do not accept the reincarnation theory.

Besides the standard programme of prayers, hymns, lectures and demonstrations, some churches devote time to spiritual healing during the service. A meditation period is sometimes included. The lecture may be delivered by a medium who goes into trance, in which case the lecture supposedly emanates from some spirit guide who has taken over. In addition, Spiritualists often organise circles in their own homes. These are known as home circles, private circles or closed circles, and are more numerous and widespread than the churches themselves. In every congregation there will be two or three members who conduct circles at home. It is in these private gatherings that the more dramatic psychic phenomena sometimes occur.

If you would like to develop the type of clairvoyance that Bill Rowan and other great mediums employ, it is essential to join a church — you really cannot hope to develop the ability on your own. Later on you may move away from the church, but for the moment you must work within one unless you can find a good circle independent of any church. Do not attempt to set up one of your own until you know what you are doing.

Begin by visiting every available church two or three times. Their services may vary from week to week, so you will need several visits to evaluate them. When you have found one that suits you, start going regularly to the services. In most cases there is no need to join a church formally. (In Spiritualism there is no process of vows or any ceremonies for joining.) Most churches will let you attend any activity without officially being a member of the congregation. You must, however, attend regularly.

Get to know the members, especially the leaders, so that you become familiar to everyone there. If you let people know that you are interested in developing clairvoyance, you will probably be invited to join a development class or a circle. Usually such classes meet once a week. From then on, you do not need to attend the church services so regularly, though of course you may wish to do so. Attendance at the circle will suffice for the purpose of psychic development.

Providing you have already developed your ESP, you will have no trouble in picking up impressions of spirits during the weekly meetings. You should take every opportunity to talk about these impressions — do not just keep them to yourself. Once you have developed the knack, you must practise it just as you practised the early ESP exercises. The best method is to attempt a display. Your circle may give you the opportunity to give "messages" to everyone in the group. You may also ask the church leaders if you can give the clairvoyance during a service. Do not be shy about enquiring — Spiritualists are always keen for potential mediums to come forward, though they will expect you to have given evidence that you have some awareness of the spirits before they give you the platform. A successful demonstration of clairvoyance should ensure that you will be invited to do it again.

The technique for learning to pick up spirit messages is not difficult. Once you have sat through the first meeting of your circle, you are ready to begin. During the second or any subsequent meeting, select a member of the group and see what you can pick up about him or her. If you specifically try to sense a spirit, you will probably do so. You have already learned to sense things about people, now you can use the same method to sense spirits around those people.

Your initial impressions may well be vague. You may sense only a shadowy image or an impression of a personality. Whatever you detect, mention it to the person concerned. Virtually all circles encourage their members to speak about their impressions. Often part of the meeting is set apart for such attempts. If not, ask the leader if you may speak at an opportune moment. You will probably never be refused — this is what Spiritualism is all about.

Your first attempts are not guaranteed to be successful, but they probably will be. Since Spiritualists are believing types they will almost certainly accept most things you tell them. Do not allow this acceptance to lead you astray. Remember the believing–doubting tightrope! Whatever you pick up, make it as precise as you can. If you are wrong, do not try to hide the fact. Try again. You will succeed eventually. Of course the whole thing depends upon your having learned to use ESP in the first place. If you have not you can sit in a circle for ever and never sense anything, and many Spiritualists do just that. Some Spiritualists seem to have a blind faith that just sitting in a circle will give you the opportunity to practise spirit contact, but it will not open up psychic doors that are not already open. This is the reason that, with occasional exceptions, few circles ever produce any good clairvoyants.

The Spiritualists are unlikely to give you any encouragement towards improving the accuracy or comprehensiveness of your perceptions — this you will have to do yourself. Most Spiritualists will let you ramble on in any old fashion, so you must exercise discrimination. The circle will give you the opportunity to practise and the right environment to do it in. The actual development is up to you. There are Spiritualists who understand the principles set forth here; and there are circles where the members do have discrimination and understanding. Unfortunately they are so rare that you are not likely to find one.

After your first few attempts you will find that you can sense information about a spirit as easily as you initially detected the spirit. Select someone, pick up whatever spirit is around him or her and keep your mind open to find out more. Extra facts, images, even words and sentences will start to come. The door that you opened with tasseomancy is opening wider, letting all sorts of information through. Be sure to tell the person what you have sensed; never keep it to yourself. There may be occasional mistakes, but you will usually find you are correct.

When you have reached this stage you are ready to undertake a public demonstration. The best way to do this is to volunteer for the church service. If this is not possible try to organise things so you can spend time giving messages to several people in the circle one after the other. The idea is to practise your ability on as many people as possible.

Getting up in front of an audience to demonstrate your clairvoyance is the best possible way to develop it. Indeed, it is the only way to increase your awareness of the spirit world once that awareness has begun. It does not matter whether the audience is a congregation in a church, a circle of Spiritualists or simply a group of people; although the advantage of a congregation is that the members are sympathetic and attentive. While it is certainly possible to practise Spiritualistic clairvoyance for a single client, the best way to develop your skills is to perform for a group.

You may be wondering why all this has to be done within a Spiritualist group. If so much depends on your own efforts, why not do it all by yourself? The answer is that spirits really do seem to congregate around the churches and circles, and it seems to be far easier to make psychic contact with spirits here than elsewhere. This fact supports the proposition that the spirits are real. If it is just a matter of picking things out of a person's subconscious memories, why should this be relatively easy in a Spiritualist gathering and relatively difficult outside? Spiritualists believe that spirits tend to be attracted to their meetings. Perhaps it is true; it certainly seems to be.

You will find that your successes are greatest when you work from a Spiritualist platform during a service. Although my own ESP is good, all my most dramatic spirit contacts have occurred during church services. There is definitely something about these meetings that stimulates and facilitates the Spiritualist form of clairvoyance. You will also find that the larger the congregation, the better your results. Even the best mediums seldom shine in small gatherings, while the really big public meetings nearly always provide good displays. The Spiritualists believe it is because power is drawn from the people present, so that the more people there are, the more power there will be. As explained previously, using ESP is easier with strangers than with people you know. So another disadvantage of a small group is that you are more likely to know some of the people, while in a large audience there are sure to be a number of strangers.

Once you have got the basic ability, it will remain with you even when you are not in contact with the church. Spiritualists say the spirits are attracted to good mediums, just as they are attracted to the churches. A more likely explanation is that once you have the ability you can exercise it anywhere. Nevertheless, it still works best in a Spiritualist environment.

There are two rules to remember when demonstrating Spiritualist clairvoyance. Firstly, always announce everything you pick up, no matter how improbable it may seem. Give your first impressions, do not try to modify or rationalise them. The rational part of your mind will only hinder the free flow of your impressions. This rule applies to any sort of ESP, and it is particularly important in Spiritualistic demonstrations. Second, always have the person to whom you are speaking answer back. It does not matter what he or she says, as long as something is said. The sound of his or her voice plays a strong part in strengthening your spirit contact. Spiritualists point out that nobody would talk into a telephone if the person on the other end refused to reply. A spirit wanting to contact someone tries harder if that person responds. Certainly, all clairvoyants find that the sound of a person's voice seems to stimulate their psychic perception. On the other hand, unsuccessful Spiritualist clairvoyants often ignore this rule. Having no real ability, they never realise the importance of the voice. They rattle on, giving one foolish message after another, never bothering to get a response from the people they speak to.

It is possible that the Spiritualist interpretation of this rule is not correct. It may be that the sound of a voice somehow stimulates ESP, regardless of whether there is a spirit present. Perhaps this contributes to the phenomenon of "phonevoyance" mentioned in the previous chapter. Another relevant fact is that some psychics have produced brilliant results on the telephone while working on radio or television shows. David Hoy, the American psychic, devoted years to appearing on talk-back television programmes, giving psychic answers to questions posed by viewers. Other psychics have found that their ESP seems to function best under these conditions. Part of the effect is no doubt due to the enormous size of the audience. Perhaps the fact that the psychic is working with voices over the phone helps, too. Whatever the explanation, always remember to get a vocal response from anyone for whom you attempt a reading.

Spiritualists have noticed that spirits often say the same sorts of things. You will find that when you tune in to a spirit, its usual reaction is, "Hello", or "I'm pleased to meet you". Indeed, sometimes this is all that the spirit seems capable of communicating. Another common reaction is, "I'm alive!". So many spirits of people who have died seem astounded to discover that they live on after death. These simple human reactions are not at all impressive from the point of view of an audience, but such reactions are to be expected, nonetheless.

Spirits often comment on possessions they have left behind them. If you happen to have a ring belonging to your dead father, and a Spiritualist tells you the spirit of your father is present, he is almost sure to comment on the ring. Photographs and jewellery are frequently mentioned. Other members of the family are commonly mentioned too. A curious case of this type occurred during a demonstration from Bill Rowan. He was talking to an old woman, telling her the spirit of her mother was present. After several comments, Bill remarked that she was wearing a cross on a chain around her neck, hidden under her dress. She admitted she was wearing such a cross. He then said, "Your mother says you have another cross at home".

"Oh, no," replied the woman.

As Bill has the ability to visualise the inside of a person's home, he began: "If I stood in front of your house, the entrance is on the left-hand side. Behind the front door is a passageway. At the bottom of the passage are two rooms. In the room on the right-hand side there is a wardrobe against the wall, a dresser and a bed under the window. In the dresser are three drawers. In the second drawer down . . . "

"Oh, yes!" exclaimed the woman. "There *is* another cross in that drawer." The audience murmured appreciatively.

"Well," said Bill, "your mother wants you to wear that cross."

"Oh, I couldn't do that," she replied, smiling.

"Why not?"

"It's a big cross. It came off the wall of a church!" The congregation, along with Bill, dissolved into laughter. Obviously, brilliant as Bill's clairvoyance was, it was not quite perfect.

The very best of the Spiritualistic clairvoyants have always been natural psychics who possessed strong ESP from childhood. It is unlikely that you will ever attain the remarkable standards of the top mediums in the world. However, it is certainly possible for anyone with ESP to achieve a good degree of spirit contact. In London there is an organisation known as the Spiritualist Association of Great Britain (SAGB) where mediums and clairvoyants are trained for the work. Here is a case that I witnessed from one of the training sessions.

In a large meeting room three student mediums were at work before an audience, under the guidance of an experienced teacher. Each of the students would select someone and speak to him or her for a few minutes, describing a spirit. The teacher would then require another student to take over and continue to provide information about the same spirit. The idea was for all the students to learn to tune in to the same spirits, thus proving that three mediums could independently communicate with someone in the spirit world. The teacher provided a good deal of guidance along the way.

One of the students spoke. "I see an old lady beside you who is very anxious to communicate. She was around all the time when you were a child, but she seems to have been a distant relation. She wasn't a close relative, but she looked after you and was very fond of you."

"Oh, yes, that's my Great-aunt Ruth," said the man to whom she was speaking. "She was like a second mother. She was a marvellous person."

"She's smiling and nodding her head. She seems absolutely delighted to have contacted you. She tells me you lived near a lake."

"That's right," said the man.

"There was a boating shed and a boat and you used to go on picnics together. She says, do you remember the time you left your hat on the island?"

"It wasn't a hat," said the man with a laugh. "It was half my clothes. I was in my bathing suit and my father was furious with me for leaving the stuff behind."

The student made a few more comments and then added, "She wants to say something about a picture". The man had nothing to say about this. At this point the teacher chimed in and took over.

"The picture she's talking about is a very valuable one that belonged to her. It's in your home now."

"Oh, yes," said the man. "It's funny, I was thinking about that picture just this week."

"She is saying that she wants you to get it reinsured. It's undervalued at present and she wants you to increase the insurance."

"Why, that's extraordinary!" exclaimed the man. "That's exactly what I was doing this week." The audience broke into spontaneous applause. This episode was easily the most impressive of the evening and was an outstanding example of Spiritualism at its best. But this was not one of the world's top mediums at work, merely a student and a conscientious teacher doing their best to provide evidence of life after death. There should be two questions in your mind about this story: firstly, was the whole thing "set up" with a man planted in the audience? And secondly, were the mediums really seeing and talking to a spirit or merely picking memories out of the man's mind?

In reply to the first question, I would advise you always to suspect fraud if you encounter such a case. There are occasions when fraudulent performers do use tricks and secret methods to make it seem like they are psychic. However, I have seen cases of this sort occur literally hundreds of times with hundreds of different people, under circumstances which preclude the possibility of fraud. I also have the ultimate proof, and that is that I can do it myself. And I believe that anyone with ESP who sets about Spiritualism the right way can learn to do it as well. There are countless numbers of Spiritualists who never achieve these sorts of results. But at the SAGB, and in certain other churches in almost every country, there are Spiritualists who strive for accuracy and who succeed in achieving it. I have personally known two Spiritualists who, starting with no ESP at all, practised for many months until they eventually succeeded. Obviously there must be many others who have done the same. In Chapter Seven there is information about psychic fraud. Certainly you need to be on your guard for it if you investigate psychic subjects. Your best safeguard is simply to investigate anything that looks suspicious. You can soon decide for yourself whether your suspicions are justified. The best method of all is to practise ESP yourself so that you know it is genuine.

The second question, whether it is really spirit contact or simply ESP at work picking memories from someone's mind, is a difficult one. Bill Rowan and I often discussed the problem of *proving* which one is really at work in any given case. In the long history of Spiritualism there have been cases where telepathy was ruled out because no living person knew the information which the spirit provided. If you read widely or investigate Spiritualism deeply sooner or later you will come across such cases yourself. However, since the purpose of this book is to show you how to develop your ESP, the issue of proving life after death is not of vital importance. When you have learned to perceive the spirit world yourself, you can do your own research to find out how much of what you pick up is telepathy and how much is actually coming from the spirits. For the moment, concentrate on learning to contact the spirits in the first place.

Among the Spiritualists, you will encounter many other phenomena besides clairvoyance. Many of these will not help you to develop your ESP and should be avoided. Foremost among these is trance. Every church seems to have three or four members who can go into a trance. To date, I have never seen anything psychic come out of these trance states and I have witnessed a great deal of total nonsense put forward by entranced mediums.

It is not difficult to learn to pass into the trance state. Many circles are devoted to teaching people how to do it. Keep away from them — it is not a worthwhile activity. When in trance a medium appears to be taken over by another personality which is invariably considered to be a spirit. The "spirit" will then speak, move around and carry out all sorts of actions while the medium remains totally unconscious. On awakening he or she will generally have little or no memory of what has just taken place.

Usually the "spirit" has distinctive mannerisms. It may claim to be a child or of a foreign nationality. Red Indians, Zulus, funny Irishmen and other characters, who appear to have stepped from the pages of a second-rate play, are frequently encountered. Curiously the Chinese guides never speak Chinese nor do the Zulus comprehend any African language, though occasionally they spout gibberish which is supposedly their native tongue. Arabs, Tibetans, Atlanteans and all sorts of exotics continually turn up as "spirit guides". Another common character is the "Highly Evolved Soul" from a higher sphere who insists on being treated as a great teacher though he or she cannot seem to utter a gramatically correct sentence.

None of it is real. The trance is genuine, but all that is happening is that the subconscious mind of the medium is having fun role-playing. Two types of communication tend to come through: one is speeches about love, brotherhood and other idealistic notions; and the other is speeches on the nature of the universe and the history of the world. The latter are particularly popular with certain Spiritualists and are often published in book form. When Blavatsky produced her almost unreadable *Secret Doctrine* or Jane Roberts issued her multi-volumed *Seth Material*, there were always readers who considered the results as the marvel of the century. A characteristic of these effusions is that they are invariably voluminous. Another characteristic is that they all contradict each other.

Spiritualists and other occultists tend to believe that the "guide" is just what it claims to be, but psychologists who investigate are seldom convinced. Nevertheless, there are a few occasions when the trance state produces something interesting. "Silver Birch" and "White Eagle" are two twentieth-century spirit guides whose speeches have been published. Many readers agree that their language is beautiful. Others have found the teachings to be helpful and uplifting. These and a few others are the cream of the crop. Unfortunately the great bulk of messages from the trance state never approaches this standard. Even with Silver Birch and White Eagle there is nothing psychic or extrasensory about their production.

There are also isolated cases of trance mediums being taken over by the spirits of the recently dead. Mrs Piper, the most famous American medium, convinced many scientists that she was bringing through real people not long passed away. Friends of the deceased, on sitting with the entranced medium, came away convinced. The spirits were able to give their names with complete details of their lives and could converse naturally with the friends who attended the seances. Most trance mediums are nothing like Mrs Piper. It may be fun to sit in the dark and listen to a "spirit" orate on the history of Atlantis or lecture on the power of divine love, but there is nothing psychic about it. Going into trance or listening to a trance speaker will do nothing to develop your ESP. My advice is to leave it alone.

Automatic writing is closely related to trance work. The medium does not lose consciousness, but he or she does remove consciousness from his or her hand, which holds a pen. Soon the pen begins to scribble, then perhaps to write. The writing corresponds to what is heard from a trance speaker and entire books have been produced in this manner. But there is a real danger with automatic writing — a few people who practise it have started to lose control of themselves. Their personality gets taken over by the "spirit", resulting in a schizophrenic breakdown. What is really happening is that the conscious mind is being overwhelmed by the subconscious. Whatever you want to call it, this is a very distressing experience. There are also people who find that automatic writing releases thoughts from the subconscious that are better left at rest. Sexual tensions, repressed anger, negative emotions that have been buried in the subconscious may come bubbling up through the writing. Many a religious or spiritually inclined person has been shocked to discover that his or her automatic writing produces a mass of obscenity or blasphemy.

The ouija board is a more clumsy method for achieving similar results. Spiritualists believe that the little pointer on which one's fingers rest moves under the influence of the spirits. Psychologists know that it is merely unconscious movement produced by the fingers. It is extraordinarily rare for anything of value to come through a ouija, although, as with automatic writing, there are exceptions. The ouija may be bought as a commercial "Ouija Board" or can be made by upending a glass on a table on which the letters of the alphabet have been arranged. The dangers of automatic writing are not as prominent when using a ouija board, yet it is prone to producing similar rubbish. As with the other automatic phenomena, there is no connection with ESP or psychic development.

All of these activities are sidetracks. At best they may prove interesting; at worst they can be dangerous. Outstanding results are so rare that it is scarcely worth involving oneself with them. A good rule with any type of seance is to begin with a prayer. I recommend this whether or not you believe in the spirits, and regardless of your religious opinions. Pray for safety and security, pray that no harm may come to you and that your efforts may produce good. Whatever your own beliefs, such a prayer acts as a mental focus which goes a long way towards ensuring your safety in whatever follows. Some Spiritualists neglect this rule, believing that their church or their circle is always under the protection of God. This is foolish. Every attempt to contact spirits should be opened and closed with prayer as a matter of course.

This brings us to the most important question of all about Spiritualism: is it worthwhile? If you are interested in expanding your psychic perception, the answer must be yes. Spiritualism will not teach you to be psychic, but it can widen your psychic awareness. The sort of impressions you can learn to receive through Spiritualism are in a different class from anything you can gain on your own. As a means of gaining conviction about life after death, Spiritualism is unparalleled. Along with all the mistakes and false ideas there are many opportunities for finding proof that life goes on after the grave. If you have doubts about this it may take you a year or two of searching, but your chance of finding the required evidence is very high.

Finally there is the religious aspect of Spiritualism. Never forget that Spiritualism is a religion and that the Spiritualists believe in it. To many the prayer, worship and meditation of a Spiritualist church are a satisfying alternative to the rigid theology and ritual of the other churches. Spiritualists are sincere folk and are easy to befriend — respect their beliefs if you go among them.

Spiritualism has its faults, chief among them being ready acceptance of everything remotely connected with the psychic world. However, Spiritualism has offered more to psychical research in the way of evidence of phenomena than all the parapsychological laboratories put together. It is worth investigating.

Chapter Five
WHAT ABOUT CARDS AND STARS AND PALMS?

Take a look at the personal advertisements in your local newspaper. Chances are you will come across ones like these from my Toronto paper:

- Palm- and card-reader guarantees to tell your future.
- Mrs Zona: psychic palm- and card-reader ... one visit will convince you.
- Well-known Astrologer: also tarot and palm-reading. Reasonable rates.
- Mother Ziska, amazing psychic. Tells past and future. Palm, cards, teacups, dreams and lucky numbers.

These are all professional readers, claiming to have extrasensory powers. North America is riddled with them, so is Europe; Britain has fewer or, perhaps, her psychics are not quite as blatant. In America magazines like the *National Enquirer* carry advertising from dozens of psychics, all of them vying with each other for your dollars.

On many occasions journalists have investigated these readers and exposed most as downright charlatans; yet they continue to flourish. One reason for this is that, in addition to the con artists, there are always genuine psychics who help maintain the public faith. The best of the world's astrologers, palmists, graphologists, etcetera often show evidence of having ESP. This raises the question: does the study of astrology or any other occultism somehow stimulate ESP? Or are these subjects merely props used by the frauds for a quick buck? In this chapter there will not be any instructions on how to read hands or horoscopes. Instead we will examine the link between these subjects and your own ESP.

Astrologers will tell you that astrology is a science. It is based upon mathematics and many years of study are devoted to learning the rules and calculations for drawing up a horoscope. Nevertheless, few practitioners will deny that intuition or ESP play a part in their success. The best astrologers are often said to be psychic. Clients may refuse to believe that results come entirely from the study of the stars, although this is what the astrologers maintain. Can it be that years of study have somehow stimulated the latent ESP of the astrologer? Or is it possible that the only successful astrologers are those who had ESP to begin with?

Finding a competent astrologer is far easier than locating a good clairvoyant. I have never lived in a city which lacked well-respected astrologers. In places such as New York or London hundreds may be found. Astrology has boomed for the last 50 years, and its history stretches back over 2000 years. It is no wonder these practitioners are fairly numerous.

You may completely disregard the daily or weekly newspaper "horoscopes". They have no connection whatever with real astrology. It is amazing that anyone believes in them, yet apparently a proportion of readers does. I would also advise you to avoid the astrologers who write these columns, tempting though a personal consultation might seem. As a group, astrologers tend to be sincere, intelligent, knowledgeable people. Unlike the rest of the psychic field, which is rife with cranks and frauds, astrologers are nearly always honest people. Of the few exceptions I have met, most were the authors of a regular astrology column! Though I hasten to add that a few of these were certainly respectable, I regret that the majority were not. Real astrologers know that the horoscope columns are completely invalid. It follows that any astrologer who writes one is abandoning the truth for money. Alternatively, he or she may be such a poor astrologer that he or she cannot tell the truth from falsehood.

You should also avoid anyone who advertises astrology along with palmistry, tarot reading, numerology, etcetera. Many astrologers have studied some of these occult "sciences" as side interests. Experts never claim to specialise in them all, but dabblers love to advertise that they practise in several fields. The real astrologer advertises as an astrologer, not as an astrologer-palmist-numerologist, even if he or she does know something about these subjects. To advertise in multiple fields indicates a lack of specialisation and probably an inflated ego.

Astrologers begin a reading by taking your date, time and place of birth. With the aid of mathematical tables known as ephemerides, the astrologer then calculates the position of the sun, the moon and the planets at that exact moment in time. It is all very methodical. There appears to be no room for ESP in the process. Why then do so many people claim that ESP enters the picture?

A horoscope contains dozens or even hundreds of factors. Each planet may be in a different sign of the zodiac and in a different house (section of the chart). The angle between any pair of planets is constantly changing as they move and all these angles are taken into account. The planets rise, set and change position, forming countless patterns, all of which have separate meanings.

An astrologer must be familiar with every one of these factors in order to interpret a chart.

Many students of astrology may learn the rules yet not succeed in putting them all together. Such a student will erect a chart, state certain facts, yet be unable to combine them for a satisfactory conclusion. On the other hand, a gifted student takes one look at the chart and instantly sees what it all means. Perhaps these successful astrologers have a gift for synthesising information that the others lack. A more likely explanation is that their intuition is well developed — it is this that enables them to make sense from a mass of facts. The best astrologers do seem to have this intuitive "feel" for interpreting charts.

There is a branch of astrology that depends almost entirely on this special intuition. It is called "horary astrology". With this method the astrologer does not work from your birth data, but from the exact moment at which you consult him or her with a question. Before 1900 horary astrology was used very extensively. In India it is still much used today, but only a handful of western astrologers employs it. Obviously horary astrology cannot be scientific. No-one would believe that the planets arrange themselves to answer any trivial question at any time you care to ask it. Horary astrology can only succeed if the astrologer is highly intuitive.

The most famous American astrologer of all time, Evangeline Adams, worked entirely with horary astrology. Her clientele included politicians, industrialists and the most influential people in America during the 1920s and 30s. Adams always swore that her astrology was a science, but no other astrologer came close to her success. It is likely that psychic awareness was the key that enabled her to perform brilliantly.

Scientific research has been carried out into the validity of astrology with mostly negative results. Hundreds of research projects have been undertaken at various times. In most cases the rules of astrology were either disproved or the tests failed to find any evidence to support them. All of these projects are summarised in a book by Dr Geoffrey Dean, *Recent Advances in Natal Astrology*. Although there is some scientific support for some branches of the subject, much of traditional astrological theory has been shown to be completely unscientific.

While much of what astrologers believe has been proven to be untrue, however, there are astrologers who are usually correct in their interpretations. Clearly some degree of ESP must be at work. In his book Dean tells an amusing story of three astrologers who each employed different, conflicting systems. The three were invited to test their systems by stating what had happened to a certain man on a particular day in the past. It was the day that his father had died. Although the three used disparate systems, two concluded that the man had lost a parent and the third that he had lost his father. Each astrologer regarded this as proof that his own system was right. It is more likely that the real answer is that ESP, and not astrology, was responsible for the results.

I have known a great number of astrologers and my opinion is that the successful ones used ESP. It also seems likely that this is true for the best astrologers everywhere. While a detailed knowledge of astrology plays a part, psychic awareness plays a bigger one. This principle also applies to professionals in other fields. Among doctors, there are always those who excel at diagnosis. Other medical people, equally learned, never do as well. A small proportion of stockbrokers persistently predict market fluctuations far better than their competitors. Of all the garage mechanics you meet, you will note that a few find your car's problem at first inspection, while the rest will still be working on it three days later. It seems to me that these people all have two things in common: they possess a good deal of knowledge combined with a deep interest in their work. These factors together promote the use of ESP. These experts do not receive "psychic flashes" the way that you have learned to. Having never learned to open their psychic perception, their ESP has to work in a more indirect manner. It *guides* them in selecting the right answer from all the possible ones. The astrologer who picks the one important fact out of a horoscope may believe he or she is exercising skilled judgement. In fact, his or her extrasensory perception is guiding that judgement without any conscious awareness. The doctor, the mechanic or stockbroker are experiencing the same effect in their decision-making. So although astrology has no direct link with ESP, a deep study of astrology may stir up one's extrasensory powers which can then aid one in interpreting horoscopes. Whatever your line of work the same effect is possible. Since there are far simpler ways to stimulate ESP, there is really no need to go about it in this way. It is easier to stay with the programme given in Chapter Three.

Palmistry is another field long favoured by amateur psychics. They seem to think that staring at someone's hands is more impressive than staring at cards or a crystal ball while waiting for impressions to come through. These people are not reading hands at all. They might as well be examining your toenails for all the difference it makes. Real palmistry is something altogether different. Like astrology, it claims to be a science. You can learn it from books or from an experienced teacher like those of Britain's Society for the Study of Physiological Patterns. Contrary to popular belief, palmistry is not simply "palm-reading". The lines in the hand are only a part of what the palmist studies. Equally important are the shape of your fingers, thumbs and the overall form of your hand. Modern palmists study fingerprints for information on your inherited (genetic) make-up.

Genuine palmists are very rare. There are several hundred times as many astrologers as there are palmists. Nearly all the "palm-readers" who advertise as such know nothing about real palmistry. Consequently, the public fails to realise that such a thing as genuine palmistry exists. For this reason real palmists often advertise as "cheirologists" or "hand analysts" to distinguish themselves from the fraudulent palmists. Another term used by the few experts in this field is "scientific palmistry".

Scientific palmistry began in France in the 1840s and has been steadily revised and improved since that time. It is best established in England. Palmists proliferate in India and Asia, though they are seldom scientific. Palmistry claims to be mainly a system for analysing character and health, but it also claims that major events of your past and future are mapped out in your palm rather than the day-to-day events which a psychic picks up.

The best palmists, like astrologers, show signs of being psychic. Indeed, the parallels between astrology and palmistry are so close that most of what I have said about astrology can equally be said of palmistry. It has no direct link with ESP; however, certain psychics claim that they can sense things more easily from the hands than from any other part of the body. There is an occult tradition that the hands radiate energy which can be used for psychic healing. If this theory is true it may explain why some people find that touching or looking at your hands conjures up a stream of psychic impressions. I think this is a matter of personal belief — having once found that he or she can sense things from your hands, a psychic may become convinced that this is the only way to do things. Such a belief is a restriction on your own ESP and should be avoided.

There is also an element of pretence in claiming to be a "palmist" when you are really practising ESP. Some psychics and many pseudopsychics like to have a prop to appear knowledgeable or specially talented. Reading hands can be such a prop. The great rule with all ESP development is to balance openness with honest doubt or criticism. To pretend to be something you are not would be a violation of this rule. So do not try "palm-reading" unless you really want to study the science of palmistry.

The crystal ball is another item used more often as a prop than a real psychic tool. I have known psychics who claim to use a crystal to "pick up impressions", whereas the true crystal-gazer does no such thing. He or she sees visions in the crystal. He or she does not "pick up impressions" the way a psychometrist does. I have never, ever met anyone who learned to see visions in a crystal. The very few people who can see such visions all have an innate ability to do so. It is not something you can learn, in spite of the various books that claim to teach you how. People who have this ability do not require a crystal — a glass of water or a blank television screen will get results just as well. For such people a crystal ball may be a useful tool. For any other would-be psychic a crystal ball is merely an attractive and expensive plaything.

The few scientists who have studied crystal-gazing have concluded that the phenomenon is not a psychic one. The visions that a scryer (crystal-gazer) sees do not necessarily relate to the past or the future of anyone else. They are simply mental pictures, similar to dreams. A person who can see such pictures might possibly be able to train himself or herself so that the visions relate to past and future events. If you have the gift of scrying, by all means try. For most of us who do not have the gift, there is little point. Buying a crystal will not strengthen whatever ESP you have nor enable you to see visions.

Card-reading bears no resemblance to astrology or palmistry. Known as cartomancy, divination by cards is probably the world's most widespread form of fortune-telling. It has features that deserve special attention. Three separate phenomena play a part in card-reading, whether it is done with humble playing cards or with the more prestigious tarot pack. Firstly, the cards themselves tend to fall into meaningful patterns. Second, there is a technique for laying out and interpreting the cards. Third, the cards may stimulate psychic impressions in the mind of the reader.

The first of these is the most surprising. When you shuffle a pack of cards, then lay them out, the result is never a random pattern. Instead, cards that really do apply to the question you have asked often turn up. This phenomenon occurs with standard card-players as well as with card-readers. Every poker player knows that runs of luck often happen during a game. A machine, designed to shuffle cards, might always produce a random result, but not so with people.

Here are just a few examples of the many I have seen. A young man asked me what I could tell him about a relationship he had recently established. He shuffled my tarot pack and, at my instructions, selected three cards which he placed face up on the table. The central card, representing the essential answer to his question was number six, "The Lovers". There are 78 cards in the pack. He had drawn the one card that most closely related to his question.

This type of coincidence occurs frequently. It is the rule, rather than the exception, when working with cards. One could write a book on this phenomenon alone. It is one of the few occult effects that is so common, so repeatable, that anyone can verify its existence. Players of card games are as familiar with it as any cartomancer. While serving in the Australian army, I played the game "500" with a group of friends over a period of several months. One of the soldiers, Harry Reimesmar, a man whose life contained many psychic experiences, swore that he could mentally force the dealer to deal him aces. One day we tested him and found that it was true. Over a dozen games he managed to receive twice as many aces as any other player no matter who was dealing. Thereafter few of the other soldiers cared to play when Harry was taking part.

On another occasion a friend asked me to help her select the tarot card which best represented herself. Technically such a card is known as the Significator. To find this card we made a series of 100 readings and carefully noted which cards turned up in the Significator's position. According to chance every card in the pack should have come up once or twice in this position. In fact only a handful of cards ever did so and, of these, one card occurred twice as often as any of the others. Naturally we concluded that this was the card she should adopt. The statistical probability for this happening is very small.

There are several possible explanations why this phenomenon takes place. A popular theory is that when you shuffle the cards you are unconsciously arranging them in the right order. An expert cardsharp might have trouble doing such a thing, but this theory holds that your subconscious mind can do it automatically. The theory collapses when someone else shuffles the cards and then you lay them down. The results are the same as if you had done the shuffling. If it were true that only you know the cards' meanings, the other person's subconscious can hardly have stacked the deck. I have sometimes shuffled the cards without knowing what question was being asked and then deduced the question by studying which cards came up in the reading. No amount of subconscious arranging could account for this.

Arthur Edward Waite, creator of the most popular modern tarot deck, believed that spirits of some sort influence the cards. He called them "elementals", which is only another name for what

was once known as fairies. While I am inclined to believe that
there are spirits around us, I find it difficult to accept that they
spend their time playing amateur cardsharps.

The famous psychologist Carl Jung postulated a law he named
"synchronicity". He suggested that just as there are natural laws
like the law of gravity, so, too, there is a law that creates
coincidences. When Mr Henry R. Zadbecker smashes his car into
Mr Robert H. Zadbecker (a type of coincidence occurring many
times in recent years), Jung would say that this is synchronicity
at work. The theory proposes that all sorts of random happenings
are inclined to come together so that they appear to be related,
even though there is no real connection between them.
Synchronicity, then, would explain why cards turn up in
meaningful patterns.

Yet another explanation is that it is all due to telekinesis. The
parapsychologists have coined this word to describe mind over
matter. One researcher into psychic phenomena, Dr J. B. Rhine,
experimented with people who believed they could influence the
way that dice fall. He found that some people could do this
merely by concentrating. Movement of objects may take place
during seances or poltergeist outbreaks, but very few people can
voluntarily move a stationary object. Rhine found several people
who could influence the dice when the dice were falling, but not
when the dice were standing still. It is possible that when the
cards are being shuffled, telekinesis is at work arranging them.
Whatever the answer, the fact remains that card-reading does
include this phenomenon.

The second phenomenon is the interpretation of card patterns.
There are plenty of books that will show you ways to do this.
Most books on cartomancy give you a variety of "spreads" you
can use. They range from simple techniques, using only one or
two cards, to very complex ones using two or more packs. You
have to memorise not only the meanings for each card but also
the meanings of positions and combinations of cards. These rules
correspond roughly to those an astrologer uses in interpreting a
chart. The major difference is that any cartomancer can make up
his or her own system. Card-readers swear that some systems are
better than others. The favourites are often jealously guarded,
passed on to privileged disciples or sold for large sums of money
to eager students. Teachers of cartomancy often concentrate on
describing the shades of meanings for each particular card rather
than giving general instruction about techniques.

The most detailed system ever published was produced by an
American woman, Catherine Sabin. Her book, *The Cybernetic
ESP Breakthrough*, sets it out. Sabin reasoned that most systems

are traditional and old fashioned and that we needed a modern, scientifically designed system of card-reading. If such a system were made very complex, it could then deal with any possible question or any sort of intricate problem. Accordingly she created a method that is quite comprehensive and yet so orderly that it is not difficult to understand. It takes weeks to master, but it is worth the trouble. I strongly recommend this book, not just because of the system but for the many interesting suggestions and wise advice given. Catherine Sabin has much to say on the technique of giving readings along with her marvellously complicated system.

There is a theory that if you memorise a set of symbols you can drive them into your subconscious. Your subconscious will then start to give you messages using these symbols. One way to do this is to take a dream book and memorise all its meanings. Soon your own dreams will contain the symbols from the book. It does not matter which dream book you choose, as long as you study it thoroughly. Similarly, if you memorise a system of card-reading, it is possible that the cards will start to turn up in ways that match what you have learned. I am not certain that this theory is correct, but I have seen some evidence to support it. It would certainly explain why cartomancers claim that the more they use a system, the better it works.

The third factor with cartomancy is the use of "psychic flashes". These are the same sorts of impressions you have learned about in the preceding chapters. Many card-readers find such impressions occur during a reading. If you have followed the exercises I recommended, you will most likely experience the same thing when you try card-reading. Just as psychometry helps the flow of ESP, so holding or just looking at cards does much the same thing. You can use a watch as a focus or you can use the cards.

The sort of free association you used in studying tea-leaves can be employed with cards, especially the tarot. The tarot cards contain many pictorial elements — each card is made up of various shapes and symbols. When you have a dozen spread out, it is possible to let your mind roam over them searching for whatever might prove relevant. I knew an amateur psychic who never bothered to memorise the meanings of the cards. He would spread out the cards and just let his imagination take over; time and again, his guesses proved right. While I do not recommend this method, my friend proved it can be done.

Louie, the card-reader you met in Chapter One, hardly bothers with a system at all — he has certain rules but mostly he just fingers the cards, waiting for psychic impressions to come through. So you see, card-reading can be quite productive for psychic work. A cartomancer who works strictly by the book will score a certain number of successes. A psychic who employs card-reading will do much better. The cards provide a useful adjunct to the extrasensory powers.

One danger needs to be carefully pointed out, however. True, the cards tend to fall into meaningful patterns; but this can be deceptive because those patterns may reflect a person's hopes or fears rather than an accurate picture of the future. When a person with business problems visits a cartomancer and the cards indicate a financial loss, this is not necessarily what lies ahead. It is more likely to be just a reflection of his or her own mind. Similarly, a person desperately in search of love and marriage is almost certain to draw cards indicating these. To the client this seems convincing; but in fact it is an illusion. Catherine Sabin discusses this in detail, suggesting various ways to overcome it. I really advise you to read her book if you plan to go far with card-reading, as I find that this problem crops up all the time. I know some readers for whom the cards do reflect the future, but for me they invariably reflect the present. Either my own views or the views of the person for whom I am reading seem to come up in the cards. Because the cards apply to the subject in question the reading looks impressive; but it is highly deceptive.

If someone asks, "Will I get married?" I can be sure my cards will reply, "You will get married". It is like an echo, very reliable, but quite untrustworthy. For this reason I seldom bother trying to forecast the future. I know that no matter how relevant the cards seem to be, they are not to be trusted. You must be wary of this effect if you read cards yourself or have someone read for you. The phenomenon does affect some readers more than others but all readers are affected to some degree.

Since the 1960s the mysterious tarot cards have become more popular than the familiar playing cards. No doubt the fact that they are attractive-looking has contributed to this, as well as the aura of mystery attached to them. These cards are highly symbolic and symbols influence the deep parts of your mind. This area, the subconscious, may have its hidden abilities stirred by using the tarot.

Sabin tends to dismiss symbolism. She feels that a scientifically designed system of positions and meanings will always prove more reliable than archaic symbols handed down from antiquity. Few cartomancers agree with her. People argue over which tarot pack is the oldest or the most authentic. There is little point in such debates — if you feel happier using one particular deck, then do so, regardless of whether it is ancient or

modern. The one exception is Aleister Crowley's tarot which I
would caution against using. Crowley designed the cards to have
a psychological effect on anyone using them.

The essence of Crowley's philosophy was to win power and
knowledge for himself while corrupting and harming everyone
else who came in his way. His cards emphasise lust without love,
aggression without mercy, self-indulgence without restraint.
Crowley ended his life bankrupt, diseased and addicted to heroin.
His cards are filled with "subliminal suggestions". That is,
suggestions in the cards are perceived unconsciously by those
using them. Only someone who has studied Crowley's life and
work very deeply should ever try to work with his cards. Anyone
else should leave them alone; I believe them to be genuinely
dangerous. All the other packs appear to be harmless, and if you
want to learn about them read Kaplan's *Tarot Classic*, a magnifi-
cent survey of all the major packs and the major books on the
tarot.

An important point to note about the tarot is that it is not just a
fortune-telling system. Tarot cards have several other uses. They
can be used for meditation and for visualisation exercises. Most
occultists agree that the cards form a pictorial guidebook for
certain spiritual exercises, designed to lift your consciousness to
a higher level. They can also be used in magic — various branches
of witchcraft and South American magic employ the cards to
influence the future or the present.

There are a host of other divination systems. Most of them,
like cartomancy, depend on distributing symbols in a random
pattern. In Europe dominoes have long been used in the same way
as cards for fortune-telling. In the 1970s a set of wooden chips
bearing the letters of the old Scandinavian alphabet, the Runes,
became popular. They are laid out in much the same way as
dominoes.

Geomancy is another form of divination and it works by
placing any number of ticks on a piece of paper and then counting
them. The number is used to construct a pattern of dots which
are then interpreted. In Africa similar patterns are generated by
throwing bones, stones or shells onto the ground. The ancient
Chinese method of divination, the I Ching, is not very different.
Coins are tossed or a bundle of thin sticks is picked up and
counted. From the number a pattern is built up and the diviner
looks up its meaning in a book. Carl Jung was very impressed
with the I Ching because he found that, like the cards, it tended
to give answers relevant to the questions. In fact its magical
qualities are no different from those of cartomancy. The I Ching
differs only in that the meanings in the book offer advice rather

than predictions for the future. In a way this makes the I Ching wiser or more useful than any system designed simply to reveal the future.

None of these systems has ever approached the popularity of cartomancy. They are all variations on the same theme yet cartomancy seems the most efficient. Astrology and palmistry, purporting to be sciences, have no real relevance here. Two minor branches of divination are the use of omens and gazing at abstract patterns. The Romans divined from the flight of birds, and omens are much in use today in India. In the West some people still see such things as breaking a mirror or spilling salt as omens, though others might dismiss this as superstition. Abstract patterns include the tea-leaves in tasseomancy. Throwing wax, molten lead or even a raw egg into a bowl of water have all been used. Gazing at flickering flames is another tradition. Psychiatry, sometimes labelled as "modern witchcraft", employs ink blots. It is all much the same.

I have omitted the subject of numerology. This is largely because numerologists are even more insistent than astrologers that their work is entirely scientific, with no psychic element whatsoever. I could say many rude things about numerology but there would be little room in this chapter for anything else. Let me simply state that all 15 numerology books in my library totally contradict one another. All of them are filled with generalisations that could apply to anyone or anything. The only accurate numerologist I have met readily admitted that he was highly psychic. The rest, convinced that numerology is marvellous, only convinced me that they were totally incompetent.

In this chapter I have noted all the major systems of divination and concluded that none of them really has much to do with psychic development, although many successful practitioners may be psychic. I believe that only cartomancy has something to offer. Unfortunately it suffers from the "mirror effect" which counterbalances the advantages. I can see only two benefits from using any of these systems during a psychic reading. Firstly, for a professional reader they are a way to impress a client. To lay out the cards or ceremonially consult the I Ching does have a positive psychological effect. A reader who puts on a good show will do better than one who does not, other things being equal. If the reader is not very competent such showmanship may make the difference between a successful career and failure. However, I hope that you have deduced that the best plan is to improve your ESP — then you will not have to put on a show. Secondly, using a system helps to "flesh out" a reading. Even a genuine psychic picking up all sorts of impressions may not perceive enough to fill a half-hour reading. If he or she does a conscientious card-reading, interspersed with psychic impressions, it is an honest way to fill the required time and satisfy the customer. For a non-professional reader, neither of these points applies. Accordingly I suggest that you leave these systems alone. Concentrate on the exercises for developing ESP and leave divination until you have completely mastered your own psychic perception. There is still plenty to learn about ESP as you will see in the next few chapters.

Chapter Six

PREDICTING THE FUTURE, INCLUDING WORLD EVENTS

Famous film star to marry! — Airplane disaster in the far West! — Stock market crash! — New cure for cancer!

Have you noticed how often the popular magazines carry a page of predictions such as these? Usually they are produced by the magazine's resident psychic or astrologer. Sometimes they result from an interview with some new clairvoyant who has caught the editor's attention. There are magazines that regularly devote their January issue to predictions for the year ahead.

The public rarely notices that these predictions seldom come true. Many well-known prophets go on year after year issuing predictions that never eventuate. Experienced psychic researchers may take note but the general public cannot be bothered. *Fate* magazine, America's premier psychic monthly, makes an annual review of the previous 12 months' predictions. Invariably the reviewer notes that they were nearly all wrong. Rationalist journals such as the *Skeptical Inquirer* (organ of the Committee for the Investigation of Claims for the Paranormal) also keeps track of the dismal failures of the world's best-known clairvoyants. No wonder a certain professional fraudulent psychic was moved to remark: "Never underestimate the gullibility of the public."

Yet it is possible to make world predictions that come true. The prophecy of St Malachy, a twelfth-century prediction about the lives of the popes, has proved to be more than 80 per cent accurate. Count Louis Hamon made a stunning prediction about the abdication of King Edward VIII. In 1925 he wrote:

> The current Prince of Wales will eventually fall a victim of a love affair. When he does, I predict he will give up everything, even the chance of being crowned, rather than lose the object of his affection.

Eleven years later England was rocked when the Prince of Wales, by then King Edward VIII, abdicated the throne to marry Mrs Wallis Simpson, an American divorcée.

But why are so many predictions wrong? Granted that it is possible to foresee the future, why does precognitive clairvoyance fail so often? I believe the answer lies in the nature of time itself. Every prediction carries within it the seeds of its own failure. For example, suppose you predict that someone will fall from a ladder on a certain date. That person simply has to stay away from ladders at that time. The prediction has then failed simply because your client knew about it — the future has been altered by your act of foreseeing it.

This case is clear-cut but something similar is at work with every prediction that is made. The very fact of looking into the future changes the situation. Even if the prediction comes true, it can never be quite the same as if the prediction had not been made. The point to note here is that the actual structure of time has been changed. In the case of personal predictions this hardly matters. When a psychic predicts you will get a letter from your mother, your knowing it will scarcely affect the matter. But when a world prediction is published in a newspaper, nearly everyone knows about it. In every home where that paper is read the situation is minutely changed by that fact. The cumulative effect of all these tiny changes in the structure of time is enough to alter the future so that the prediction does not come true. "But wait a minute," you say, "if everyone reads that a bridge will collapse, how can that possibly affect whether it falls or not?" The answer is that nothing is physically changed. It is time itself that has been affected.

My view is that the flow of time is made up of an infinite number of tiny incidents. Every incident is itself the result of an infinite chain of events that led up to it. Sometimes an infinitesimal change at one point will dramatically alter the future. No-one can say what moment will be of vital importance or at what point you may find that nothing you do will alter the course of events. But a private prediction does make a certain alteration in the stream of time; and predictions of world events, published in the press, make untold thousands of changes in the time stream. It is no wonder that these predictions almost never come about. There are just two ways round this problem: firstly, make sure your world prediction is not widely known; and secondly, phrase your predictions so that no-one can understand them until they are fulfilled.

This second technique is the one most successful prophets have used. Nostradamus, for example, phrased all his prophecies in cryptic language. Only when an event had occurred did people realise what he had been talking about. Unfortunately this has made Nostradamus's prophecies the happy hunting ground for nuts and crackpots of all types. Every few years some new writer turns up with his or her interpretations of what the master wrote. They twist and turn his words to suit their own fancy. Usually they ignore fulfilments that have occurred in the past, preferring to offer their own ideas about some fanciful future event. To date no-one has succeeded in correctly interpreting a Nostradamus prediction before it has happened. Hundreds of his prophecies have already come to pass, but it is only by looking back on events that we can see this.

Nostradamus has been accused of being vague, open to any sort of interpretation, but I do not believe this to be the case. His most famous prediction runs:

> The young lion shall overcome the old,
> On the field of war in single combat,
> He will pierce his eyes in a cage of gold.
> This is the first of two loppings,
> Then he dies a cruel death.

No doubt there were people who pored over that prediction, offering interpretations from the day that Nostradamus wrote it. In 1559 King Henry II of France met the Earl of Montgomery in a jousting tournament. On the second joust Montgomery's lance splintered and entered the King's golden visor. He died in great pain several days later. No-one can accuse Nostradamus of vagueness on that occasion but it is easy to see how no-one would have guessed the prophecy's meaning before the fatal event took place.

St Malachy's prophecy uses a similar technique. He was an Irish clergyman who lived in the twelfth century and he left a list of every pope to come. There are 112 altogether and each pope is described by a two- or three-word motto. Thus, the first pope was called "From the castle on the Tiber" — this was Pope Celestine II who reigned from 1143 to 1144, and the motto proved to be apt. As with Nostradamus, no-one can use the Malachy prophecy to predict who will be the next pope. Only when a new cardinal is elected to the office does the motto become clear. It is interesting to note that our present pope, Pope John Paul II, is number 110 on the list. According to the prophecy there are only two more popes to go. However, it should be noted that Malachy's prophecies are not infallible. One or two of them do not seem to fit, others must be classed as doubtful, although the majority seem accurate indeed. The last pope, Pope John Paul I, was described as "In the middle of the moon", or "Between two moons". This might refer to his extremely short reign, though one commentator pointed out that his birth occurred exactly at the mid-point between two full moons. At any rate we shall see what happens when St Malachy's list runs out.

Later in this chapter we will look at how you can use Nostradamus's technique for yourself. First, though, let us examine the whole topic of precognition. That predictions can be made at all is a mind-boggling thought. To foresee the future implies that somehow the future already exists. But how can something be said to exist when it has no physical reality? An old explanation is that prediction simply involves seeing more of a situation than others can see. For example, a man on top of a tall building looks down at the street. He sees two cars racing towards a crossing and he knows that they will collide. Yet neither driver is aware of this because they cannot see each other. The man's prediction is based on a wider view.

This analogy breaks down when one considers actual examples of predictions. Here is one that occurred to me. An amateur psychic told me I would meet shortly a young couple from Switzerland. Since I was in Australia at the time this seemed rather unlikely. Two weeks later I drove from Sydney to Brisbane, a distance of 1000 kilometres. On the way I stopped for a couple of hitchhikers. It was a young Swiss couple, as predicted. They told me that they had arrived in the country only 10 days ago, so they had not even been in Australia at the time of the prediction. At that time I had not decided the date of my own trip. No amount of "standing on top of a tall building" could have foreseen our paths crossing as they did. Some other explanation has to be found.

When I first started to study psychic readers, I noticed a number of common factors in their readings. (The most common finding is that a so-called reader has no ability at all.) Among the genuine ones their visions of the future tend to have a distinct similarity. The average prediction gives one a glimpse of the future rather than a complete view of the event — one gets only a small part of the picture. A case in point was a man who was told by a psychic that he would soon be in a place where plastic bags were scattered all about. A few weeks later his landlord gave him notice and he bunked in with a friend. On arriving at his friend's flat he discovered that the backyard was littered with plastic bags. He commented to me afterwards, "I wish the psychic had told me about getting evicted. That business about the bags was quite correct, but it was no earthly use to me!"

I have known this sort of thing to happen hundreds of times. It occurs frequently with my own psychic predictions. I once told someone that he would be bothered by a dog howling near his home. A week later his neighbour died and the man's labrador dog set up a howl for three days. Why had I foreseen the noisy dog rather than the death itself? It seems to be a trick of the subconscious mind to ensure that the predictions will not be understood before being fulfilled. Something in the psychic's mind tries to avoid the paradox that foreseeing the future changes that future by giving only a glimpse of it.

The Greek legend of Cassandra tells of a woman who could foresee the future and who was doomed to offer correct predictions which no-one would believe. The gods had granted her the gift of prophecy on condition that no-one would be able to act on what she foretold. For the practising psychic there is a way around this dilemma. If you find your predictions give you annoying glimpses only, ask yourself what each one actually means. Do not try to ascertain the meaning by reasoning it out; use your psychic perception. Making the effort will sometimes give you the answer. In Chapter Three it was suggested that making the effort to improve your accuracy brings results. This habit is one of the secrets of psychic success. Too many psychics are satisfied with what they have, and they fail to realise that striving for something better really does work. In the same way one can occasionally attempt a psychic reading on a person who seems to be blocking your efforts. Most psychics declare that they cannot read for such a person. In fact if you merely affirm to yourself, "I *can* read for this person", you will almost always succeed. That momentary extra effort is all it takes to go straight through the block.

The next common feature of predictions is that events in the near future crop up more frequently and more accurately than the more distant events. Time and again I have visited a good psychic and been told about a dozen little things for the next few weeks which subsequently proved accurate. Only occasionally does a prediction for many months ahead come about. However, these more distant predictions invariably concern major things. It is almost a rule: small things are foreseen a little way ahead while big things are foreseen well in advance. The man who got the useless clue connected with the eviction from his flat is a good example. Does this tell us something about the nature of time?

I would liken time to a tree branch with a bug crawling on it. This branch has many side branches and each of these has various twigs. An observer could note all the twigs near the bug, and could predict that the bug will crawl on some of them. The observer can also see the end of the branch so he knows the bug will eventually get there. But he does not know which particular twigs the bug will encounter on its way.

I have a theory that time is really a matrix of possibilities. Strictly speaking time is not made up of events but rather of possibilities. When any particular possibility actually manifests, we say that an event has occurred and time has passed. What happens when precognition occurs is that your psychic awareness reaches its way through the matrix of possibilities to find the ones most likely to occur. I could draw another analogy with water finding its way through a network of channels. Some channels are wide; others narrow. The water is more likely to make its way through the wide channels, but there is always a possibility it will veer to a sidetrack through a narrow channel. Like the water, your psychic perception finds its way through the matrix of possibilities that we call time, sorting out those paths that represent strong possibilities from those that are less-likely prospects. Although major events tend to be seen well in advance, you may sometimes pick them up just before they occur. When this happens the psychic impression is tinged with a quality of absolute certainty.

I knew a teacup-reader who told a client with great excitement that she was about to win the lottery. This reader insisted that the client should go downstairs immediately and buy a ticket from the nearest newsagent. Somewhat bemused, the woman did so. She won $30,000. To her credit she generously shared this prize with the teacup-reader. Afterwards the reader told me, "I *knew* she was going to win. I was absolutely certain that she had to buy a ticket right away."

I was recently speaking to a friend on the telephone and she mentioned a job she had just applied for. My ESP told me she was certain to get it. She did, one day later. Here is one more example that occurred in Canada. A journalist who had just published her first slim volume was speaking to a fortune-teller over the phone. He told her, "I can tell you with certainty that it will reach number two on the New York best-seller list". This was an outrageous prediction for an unknown Canadian writer. She is Merle Shain and her book, *Some Men Are More Perfect Than Others*, did soar to number two on the New York best-seller list, as predicted by Norman Johnstone, Canada's best-known prophet. Although it hovered for several weeks, the book did not make it to number one.

In spite of cases like these there are also times when major events spring up unexpectedly. People who go regularly to psychics are accustomed to hearing all sorts of predictions that do come about. They also report that sometimes very traumatic events occur with no warning at all, which would be nothing startling if the psychics were phoney. But it does seem strange in the case of those psychics who are regularly giving correct predictions. It is almost as if some sort of barrier exists which hides some things in the future while plainly revealing other quite insignificant events. What can it be? I suspect that in some way the "possibility matrix" is reacting to a person who interferes regularly by peeping into the future. In order to prevent major probabilities being disturbed by foreknowledge, it hides them.

This brings us to the third factor common to most psychic predictions. They are usually *wrong*, no matter how good the psychic may be. A clairvoyant may score 100 per cent on your past and present but even the best will be lucky to maintain a 20 per cent accuracy when it comes to the future predictions. Genuine clairvoyance will always pick up a certain amount about the future, but the success rate will never be as high as for past events. This is further evidence that the clairvoyant is really detecting probable future trends rather than an absolute, pre-existing future. These future probabilities will be hedged about with all sorts of minor details — twigs on the branch — which the psychic is likely to pick up. These small details give the illusion that the future must exist in minute detail. This is not so. They are merely the details that accompany the most probable future that the psychic perceives. In practice even the most probable future may fail, in which case all the details will be wrong. To return to our analogy of the flowing water, it has gone off through one of the narrower channels.

Is it possible to change the future? This depends on many factors. If there are very strong probabilities in the matrix of time, it will take an enormous effort to change things. On the other hand the small probabilities coming up in the near future may be changed by quite minor alterations to the current state of affairs. There will also be rare cases where a very minor change at a certain point will divert the entire train of events building up in the future. The problem is that no-one can recognise such critical points when they occur. Just prior to the outbreak of World War II, *Prediction* magazine asked all the best clairvoyants in Britain to assess the likelihood of war. *Prediction* is Britain's most widely read psychic journal. At that time it was just three years old. Without exception all the clairvoyants stated that no war would break out. In fact England was at war with Germany just three weeks later. This has often been quoted as proof that all clairvoyants are phoney. My view is that it shows that in the probability matrix war was very unlikely. The psychics correctly divined the probable future but on this occasion the improbable is what actually took place.

There is a supposedly true story that throws light on changing the future. An American psychic told a man that his son would be knocked down by a car on a certain crossing at a particular date. The psychic even nominated the make of car. The parents wisely kept their son away from that crossing for months after the date mentioned, but it was to no avail. Nearly a year later the boy was struck down at the crossing exactly as predicted. It may be that the psychic got his dates wrong. This is the obvious bet, but I think it is more likely that his dates were right but that when the parents tried to change the future they only partly succeeded. The accident was too deeply embedded in the future to be easily overcome — the future merely rearranged itself to bring about the accident at a later date.

Another case turned up in my army days, when a deliberate attempt to change the future met with little success. Two friends and I were sitting round one evening with another soldier who regularly experienced precognitive dreams. Like most of those who encounter this phenomenon, he had studied the question of changing the future and concluded it could seldom, if ever, be done. One of my friends produced an electric iron that was not working. He proposed to take it to pieces and then fix it, right there at the table. Immediately the precognitive dreamer spoke up, "I had a dream about this last night. We took the iron to pieces and somehow they got mixed up so we had a devil of a job getting them back together again."

Here was our chance to change the future, I thought. "All we need to do is to leave the iron there without touching it. That way, your dream about the mixed-up pieces can't come true," I announced. Naturally the soldier who owned the iron was unwilling to go along with this. I urged him to comply for the sake of the experiment and he grudgingly agreed. Another soldier got an iron for him to get on with his work. The rest of us settled down for a game of cards.

Later in the evening, when he returned the borrowed iron, the man again said he wanted to work on his broken appliance. I had difficulty restraining him, but it was all in vain. Within an hour another soldier dropped in and declared he was an electrician who could fix the iron. This time my protests went unheeded. The owner and the electrician took the iron to pieces. One of them knocked something over and they found themselves unable to reassemble the thing. The precognitive dreamer watched these proceedings with a smug smile. As the owner dragged the pieces away in a paper bag, the dreamer remarked, "I knew it. Those dreams of mine always come true. Nothing can change them." I am not convinced, but he was certainly right on this occasion.

Both private predictions and those concerning world events depend on the same psychic mechanisms. If you try to foresee world happenings you are just as likely to get only tantalising glimpses rather than the whole event. It is quite common to foresee a disaster like a train crash with no idea of the date or location. Even if every detail is correctly foreseen, the prophecy is useless. This feature of such predictions opens the way for charlatans. Any publicity-seeking fraud can predict a train crash or air disaster in the hope that one will occur later that year. It is the specific details — albeit useless ones — that distinguish the genuine prediction from the fraudulent. I once foresaw a major natural disaster for an Australian city. At the end of that year the city of Darwin was destroyed by a cyclone. While this certainly fulfilled the prediction, it can hardly be called a success since I had not determined the nature of the disaster nor the city concerned. The prediction was quite worthless.

Let us now look at how you can set about making world predictions. Once you have developed your own ESP there is no difficulty in applying it to world events. Simply set aside a little time for the effort and wait to see what impressions come into your mind. Make notes on what you perceive. I like to do this at the beginning of every year. For a few days I walk around with the thought in my mind, "I wonder what will happen this year?". I jot down my impressions in a notebook and tick them off during the rest of the year if they come true. It may help to direct your thoughts to various countries, industries or groups of people. Count Louis Hamon used to gaze at a map of the world, running his eye over all the countries. Count Hamon recorded his results in his book *Cheiro's World Predictions*. It contains several notable successes but a high proportion of total failures as well.

One thing you should not do is to concentrate on any particular famous person. This seems to encourage imagination to take over, no doubt because we all have some prior knowledge and expectations with most public characters. As you know, clairvoyance works best when your mind is completely uncluttered. Many glimpses of world events come as impressions of newspaper reports rather than the actual events. It is as if you are foreshadowing what the press will say rather than seeing the event itself. At least two precognitive dreamers I have known reported this phenomenon and I have experienced it myself. It is actually quite an old discovery. J. W. Dunne wrote a famous study of precognitive dreams, *An Experiment with Time*, in which he drew attention to the phenomenon.

Dunne dreamed of an exploding mountain in the Caribbean. His dream included the fact that 70,000 people died. Later, when he read about the destruction of the island of Martinique, the newspaper mentioned that 70,000 had died. Some years later he learned that this was a mistake and the true figure was 700,000. He had foreseen the newspaper account, complete with incorrect figure.

One precognitive dreamer even established that he foresaw newspaper accounts rather than television news reports. He was a young man who was highly interested in psychical matters and he and I made a detailed study of his precognition. He would sometimes actually dream of a newspaper page with the headline or picture quite plainly shown. We noted that these dreams invariably gave him quite trivial bits of news, often so fragmentary that he could make no sense of them till the newspaper turned up and all then became clear.

Last year I experienced a series of psychic flashes while sitting in a restaurant. A couple of bottles of wine had apparently loosened up my ESP whether I wanted it to or not. One of the flashes seemed quite bizarre. It concerned an enormous flurry of public interest in UFOs. Since I am cynical about the existence of such things, this seemed just an absurd prediction. The following day all of Sydney was flooded with posters featuring the headline of a major paper, the *Daily Mirror*. They announced new UFO sightings and the posters were creating considerable public interest. Once again, I had seen only the newspaper account of an event.

Why does anyone want to foresee world events in the first place? To the developing psychic it is an interesting thing to try, as well as giving another field in which to exercise ESP. Since it is one of the most difficult of all psychic feats, it is all the more challenging and more rewarding when it works. I think one of the reasons for the difficulty here lies in the fact that you have no personal contact with what you are predicting. With a personal reading you are intimately involved. Yet you will rarely if ever be involved in a world event. Perhaps this explains the prevalence of glimpses of newspaper reports. We do have a personal link with the newspaper when reading it.

Successful world predictions are a sure-fire way of attracting attention. For the professional psychic or the amateur who wants to establish himself or herself this is an undeniable attraction. It is a shame that so few succeed, thus adding to the general disrepute of psychic phenomena. Many well-known psychics send a page of predictions to the press, and radio and television stations several times a year. Sensational journals love to publish them and it is all good publicity. Reporters who interview psychics always like to get a few predictions to feed their readers, even if the psychic has no talent for forecasting world events. Pseudopsychics love this field — there are many ways of making fake predictions. As mentioned previously, the simplest technique is to offer plenty of colourful predictions and rely on the fact that no-one will follow them up.

Another ploy is to predict things that are likely to come true. There are society psychics who simply repeat all the gossip they have picked up about movie stars and other well-known people. Another professional fraud who claims to predict stock market trends merely studies the standard market reports before issuing his predictions. Norman Johnstone, the Canadian fortune-teller, has an amusing story of a fake prophet he knew many decades ago. This man travelled from town to town selling quack medicines and doing a few magic tricks. He would come into town and introduce himself as "Professor Smith", the famous clairvoyant. He would go to the local newspaper and provide predictions for such things as crops, weather and election results. After raking in as much money as he could, he would move to the next town for a repeat performance. Except that here he would be known as "Doctor Brown", the well-known prophet. He would issue a new lot of predictions that flatly contradicted what he had said in the last town. Using this method he made his way across the country. The pay-off came at the end of the year. When the time came he would collect all the newspaper reports of his predictions together with whatever newspaper stories happened to coincide with them. Since he continually reversed his predictions, some of them had to be correct. This then gave him a nice file of fulfilled "prophecies". Next time he toured he would adopt the appropriate name under which he had made a correct prediction and have a ready-made impressive reputation.

Another fraudulent technique is the shotgun effect. The con man issues several dozen predictions in the hope that one or two may come true. When one of these lucky hits comes up, he saves it and disregards the rest. With a little effort he can build up a nice file of "documented predictions". Yet another system is to put out predictions for things that happen all the time. The list will include assassination of a public figure, death of an elderly film star and, of course, transport disasters. The wise con man knows to wait till some such event is more or less due in a specific place. A little vagueness helps as well. On the other hand, if a prediction has a spurious appearance of being fairly specific, for example, "Elderly English film star who has starred in many comedy roles", he can afford to wait for some time for it to occur. He can always change the date on the paper in which the prediction appeared if too long a period has elapsed.

Take care not to fall into this sort of chicanery without realising it. I know sincere psychics who use the shotgun system and do not realise they are deluding themselves. Another thing to be careful about is predicting the deaths of prominent people. The human imagination seems to be rather prone to coming up with

these. There are times when one can see why these false
impressions occur. After the Iranian hostage incident several
psychics predicted the imminent death of the Ayatollah
Khomeini. The old man is still alive and kicking, despite this
wishful thinking by indignant Americans. At other times there
may be no obvious reason why your mind tells you that so-and-so
is about to die. Experience has shown that such impressions are
very unlikely to work out.

Perhaps the only exception to this rule was the death of Egypt's
President, Abdul Nasser. *Fate* magazine noted with surprise that
several psychics had foreseen his sudden disappearance from the
political scene. By contrast, when President Kennedy was
assassinated the only precognitive hint was a vague and
contradictory prediction by Jeane Dixon. Curiously, in the years
after Kennedy's death the number of prophets who claim to have
predicted the event rose year by year. By 1965 there was hardly a
fortune-teller in America who did not claim to have foreseen the
event.

In my own attempts at world prediction my most abject failure
was a prediction that the Pope would be assassinated. I am rather
glad I was mistaken. Around the same time as that prediction an
interesting partial success occurred. It was in 1982 and I was
carrying home groceries with my wife when I stopped and told
her what was flashing through my head. It concerned Margaret
Thatcher, Prime Minister of Britain. I told my wife that Thatcher
was in imminent danger, and as near as I could figure it she would
suffer an assassination attempt which would not succeed. In the
process she would lose two of her top aides. Three days after this
Argentina invaded the Falkland Islands. Mrs Thatcher was
subjected to furious abuse in Parliament and two of her top people
resigned over the issue. Obviously I had been wrong, but coming
as it did so close to the day of the invasion and ensuing events,
my prediction must have been connected.

Another false prediction that regularly crops up is the science
fiction fantasy. There are psychics who announce the Martians
are coming, a meteor is going to hit the Earth or that California
will finally slide into the sea. Generally these absurdities centre
on doom and disaster. These psychics have tapped into their own
imagination and, in particular, into that part of the imagination
that delights in pure fantasy. Predictions of general doom have
been common throughout history. New religious leaders
regularly arise to announce that the end of the world is
imminent. One nineteenth-century best-seller was entitled,
*Wonders of Prophecy which Must Shortly Come to Pass Before
1880.* A later edition changed that date to 1901. Thereafter the

author lapsed into silence. If you get an impression of disaster looming up for your city or the world, you would do well to forget it. There have been psychics who predicted general disaster, only to discover that personal disaster soon overtook them. This seems to have been a case of incorrect interpretation of what the psychic had perceived.

Let us suppose you have sat down and produced half a dozen world predictions. What are you going to do with them? If you are doing it entirely for your own amusement there is no need to do anything. However, if you propose to let others know what you have discovered you must take certain steps. You will need to get your list of predictions dated. One way to do this is to lodge a copy with some reputable body, your State or federal library or your solicitor. Alternatively, you may take your list to a Justice of the Peace for notorisation. You can try sending copies to the newspapers but there is no guarantee they will print them. Nothing would be more annoying than to send predictions to a paper that ignores them, only to have the predictions correctly fulfilled. You do need to get a confirmed date on your list to prove them genuine.

If you give predictions to a newspaper, be sure they are in writing. Keep a copy of your list. Reporters have been known to sensationalise things and you may need to prove that something printed in a newspaper was not what you said at all.

Louie Olah, the card reader mentioned in Chapter One, had an experience of this kind. It was a few years ago when the American satellite "Skylab" was due to fall out of orbit. There was considerable interest as to where Skylab would come down. Louie told some of his clients he believed it would fall in the sea off Perth, Western Australia. This prediction reached the ears of a journalist who came round to interview Louie. After writing the details, the reporter asked for more world predictions. He asked specifically about the Pope, John Paul II.

"I only know one thing about him," volunteered Louie, "and that is he will have a bullet in him before this year is out." This was many months before the assassination attempt on the Pope.

The journalist was intrigued and pressed Louie to say more, which he refused to do. The following day, Louie picked up the morning paper and this is what he read: "Local clairvoyant predicts Pope will be hit by falling Skylab."

If there are only one or two copies of your list there is no danger of disturbing the matrix of time. If they are published, however, you run headfirst into this problem. The only solution is to adopt the Nostradamus technique so that no-one knows what you are predicting — publish the predictions in cryptic language. This requires a little ingenuity as you have to phrase the predictions so they sound interesting. At the same time they should be easy to read but difficult to understand. Nostradamus used rhymes of four lines each. In 1976 I made up a set of predictions of this sort. Several of them dealt with matters that have since become commonplace. Here is an example:

Waving in the wind
The very symbol will be changed
Midst much debate and discontent
No more will Jack the Cross be seen.

I tested this on several people who had no idea what it meant. In fact it referred to the changing of the Australian flag. At the time such an idea had not been mooted. Today the issue of getting a new flag is raised continually in the press. "Jack the Cross" in the prediction is the Union Jack, featured on the current Australian flag, the symbol that waves in the wind. You can make up verses like this to disguise things you have sensed about the future. Of course you must be careful to avoid ambiguity. Strive to phrase predictions so that they become perfectly clear once they have been fulfilled. To finish this chapter here are several more prophecies of the same type. Some of these apply to my country, Australia, while others apply elsewhere. Most concern the next few years, though a few go further and one extends into the next century.

Neither seen nor used before
Not from this land, yet
Much employed here. Far
And wide. I write upon it.

Australia and the world in the next few years.

In the Place of the Wall,
The lords of the Red Stain give way.
The ancient ways return, all is changed,
Parts break away; new growths.

The world later this century.

Ho, ye prophets of Doom!
Neither Fire nor Earth
But Water wrecks the wrath
You long have dreamed of.

The world within one or two generations.

Laugh, laugh good people,
The new lord is a jester.

Australia before the end of this century.

They have left the sea
To the sea they will return
Though empty now
Yet filled in times to come.

The world before the end of this century.

The Elder ones are seen no more.	*Australia*
Darkness is gone, hardly a shadow remains.	*next century.*
Three generations hence, remembered with shame.	
Five generations, lost in the mists of time.	

In the warm place first	*Australia in*
The cracks appear	*the next 10 years.*
Not broken off, but subdivided	
The old queen's power declines.	

Save this book! Twenty years from now you can look back and see how these have worked out.

Chapter Seven
ILLUSIONS AND DELUSIONS AND HOW TO AVOID THEM

"But he seemed so honest. How was I to know he was a fake?" How often has someone exclaimed this after losing money to a con man. It would help if every swindler wore a sign saying, "Beware, I am dishonest". This is not the case, however, so it would be wise to learn to recognise some of the snares and illusions you will meet in the psychic field.

Prominent among these are the various methods and courses for psychic development which simply do not work. A good many individuals and groups run classes that profess to teach psychic abilities. All they really succeed at is to disengage you from your money, often substantial amounts. It has been said, "Those who can, do — those who can't, teach". This is certainly the case in the psychic field. A good rule with anyone who promises to teach you psychic skills is to pay him or her only after you have achieved some results. Similarly pay for a psychic reading only after the psychic has proved his or her ability.

Aura-reading lessons are a good scam. There are certainly a few people who really do see auras, but nearly all of them have the ability naturally — not one of them learned to do it by attending a course. On the other hand plenty of people who have attended such classes think they can see auras. It is an illusion. The aura is said to be a field of coloured light surrounding every human being — it can be seen only with clairvoyant sight. Various people who can see this aura have recorded their observations on it. They claim that the colour of your aura reveals your health, state of mind and many facets of your character. One thing immediately evident is that all aura seers perceive the aura differently. Books that tell you that a certain colour has a particular meaning will be flatly contradicted by the next book. This does not prove that the whole thing is a fraud; it merely shows that auric vision and the interpretation of what the clairvoyant sees vary from one person to the next. The very best book on this subject, dealing intelligently with every aspect of auric vision, is *What Your Aura Tells Me* by Ray Stanford. Stanford reviews what all other writers have said and adds anecdotes from his own experience. He comes to two major conclusions:
1.   Only a handful of people who claim to see auras can really do so. Of these few, all are artists or highly interested in art.

This implies that a strong awareness of colour is necessary for auric vision.

2. People who see auras usually pick up psychic impressions from the individuals whose aura they are studying. Often they will visualise these impressions as part of the aura. What is happening is that their psychic perception is presenting information in a visual form. This implies that at least part of what they see exists more in their own mind than as an objective reality in the aura itself.

Teachers who claim you can learn to see auras usually start by placing someone in front of a white screen. A strong light is then played on this person. Anyone looking at the person is likely to see a sort of hazy outline around the body — this is merely a trick of the eye, as can be shown by the fact that putting any large object in front of the screen produces the same hazy outline. If a coloured screen is used the hazy outline will appear in the complementary colour to that of the screen. Under these conditions the coloured band will often appear several centimetres wide. Of course the coloured effect disappears as soon as the person moves away from the screen, but most students will remain convinced that they have seen an aura.

The late Tuesday Lobsang Rampa recommended that the person being looked at should be naked. (I know at least one teacher who declared that the person should also be young and female.) Students are encouraged to concentrate on this pseudo-aura. Those who cannot detect it are encouraged to exercise their imagination and to banish doubt from their minds. With practice it is easy to convince yourself that you are seeing some sort of haze around anyone. From there it is only a step to imagining all sorts of variations in the depth and shading of what you see. In my experience people who learn like this are quite unable to get any real information from their new-found ability. I once sat in a circle where four people gave different impressions of my supposed aura and not one of them could venture an interpretation for what he or she saw. By contrast, over the years I have met three people who claim to have a natural ability to see auras which was present from birth. All three have described a distinct green tinge around me and two of them remarked that they had learned to associate this with a love of reading and learning. All the folk I have met who think they have learned to see auras describe assortments of fancy colours that have no discernible relevance to the life or personality of the person concerned. This never appears to dissuade them one jot. On the other hand the few genuine aura-readers have been able to offer valid observations about the people they study.

A professional aura-reader working under the name of "Doctor Johnathon" made up coloured charts of each client's aura. They were quite pretty but were all interchangeable. Several clients comparing notes found little difference between one chart and the next. The accompanying readings all included character analyses showing intelligence, spiritual evolution, integrity, discernment and so on.

No doubt some of my readers will disagree with me if they have been through a course in aura-reading. Let them set up objective tests to see how valid their powers really are. The Science Research Group of the Theosophical Society once did this with depressing results. The account of the experiments is to be found in their book, *Psychism and the Subconscious Mind*, published by Quest. Several people who claimed to be able to see auras flowing between two outstretched hands were tested. They were asked to look at two hands held in a closed box which had a viewing window in the top. When the hands were folded the space between them but not the hands themselves could be seen. The idea was to discover whether the aura seers could see the aura only when the two hands were in view or whether they could still see an aura when the hands were out of sight. The owner of the hands was asked to move his fingers back and forth, sometimes close together, other times wide apart. None of the aura watchers was able to report accurately. They saw all sorts of changes in the aura even when the fingers had not moved at all. At one time the subject took his hands right out of the box but the seer continued to describe the aura there. Sadly all the people with auric vision were just exercising their imaginations.

One genuine aura seer I knew worked in a psychiatric hospital. One day, walking along a corridor, he noticed an aura projecting out through the closed door of a cupboard.

"Sister Jones, is that you?" he called.

"Yes! Get me out. One of the patients locked me in here," she replied. The nurse was quite puzzled as to how he knew she was in the cupboard.

"Oh, it was easy. I could see your aura poking out," he exclaimed, leaving her even more puzzled than before. Now there was a piece of objective evidence. Another aura seer offered to demonstrate before a small psychic research group I ran. He was able to tell when one of our members passed in and out of meditation by changes in the aura. This person shifted his mind from one state to another several times and the aura-reader reported all the changes faultlessly.

Well-known medium Bill Rowan can often diagnose disease by what he sees in an aura. He is also adept at detecting emotional states by the same means. Bill is highly psychic but he is very careful to differentiate between what he sees in an aura and what he learns by psychic perception. Genuine aura-readers are few and far between. Ray Stanford found barely half a dozen in his part of the United States. Fraudulent readers and self-deluded ones are far more common. So if someone offers to teach you to see auras or you pick up a book on aura-reading, my advice is to keep away! If you must experiment in this field be sure to set up some careful tests which eliminate self-delusion and imagination.

For some reason aura-reading is often linked with the reading of past incarnations. Fascinating as reincarnation research is, this, too, is full of traps for the unwary. I have no doubt that reincarnation takes place. I believe that the days when it was simply an unproved theory are long past, and for me reincarnation is as well established as the rotundity of the Earth. Unfortunately the proof has not come from hypnotism, regression or any of the other techniques of the psychic world. All of these have proved to be largely illusory. The proof comes from the case histories of a small number of people who have natural memories of their past lives.

There have always been some people who can remember a past life; they are often children. Stories about such people have been published in magazines and books since the beginning of this century. Similar cases have been reported through the centuries from many different countries. In modern times scientists have gone to the trouble of interviewing such people and investigating what they have to say. It has been established beyond any doubt that some people do have detailed, verifiable memories of an earlier life. The most famous investigator is the psychologist Ian Stevenson. He has devoted a lifetime to this work. His first book, *Twenty Cases Suggestive of Reincarnation*, dealt with 20 cases investigated in meticulous detail. To date he has issued five volumes of reports and his co-workers have published others.

Among the fraudulent systems that purport to uncover past lives is the use of hypnotism. Many people can be hypnotised quite deeply. If such a person is placed in a trance and told to remember earlier times in his or her life, he or she will soon begin to "remember" details of a life before this one began. Nearly all such memories are simply fantasy and most are composed of incidents from books or films. Often these have been completely forgotten by the conscious mind but resurface under hypnosis. Other elements of these hypnotic illusions are built from wish-fulfilment, fears and phobias, generously laced with wild imagination.

Again and again hypnotic regression cases have been investigated and found to be false. A few others were studied and produced a handful of facts that, though vague, with a little stretching might be considered true. There are a dozen books on the market composed of sloppy "research" of this type. Only a credulous "true believer" could ever regard them as proof of anything. Very rarely has a hypnotic case been investigated and proved to be accurate. Perhaps the most interesting one was provided by the British hypnotist, Arnel Bloxham. This case was probed by the British Broadcasting Corporation for a television broadcast. A woman who recalled several successive lives was able to provide many historical details which scholars then confirmed. In contrast, another of Bloxham's cases was subjected to scrutiny and proved incapable of verification. A man who relived a life as a British seaman of the eighteenth century provided colourful and realistic descriptions which simply failed confirmation. So while hypnotism may occasionally uncover a genuine past life, in the vast majority of cases it uncovers only fantasy. Obviously it is pointless to take such "past-life readings" seriously.

A recent book discusses all the techniques for reincarnation research and concludes that only the type of investigation made by Ian Stevenson can be considered valid. The book was written by Ian Wilson and has been published under two titles: *Reincarnation!* and *Mind Out of Time*. Read it if you want to look further into this subject.

Closely allied to the use of hypnosis is the practice of relaxing deeply and slipping into a daydream. There are courses that persuade whole groups of students to lie down and practise this. Under the guidance of a leader who encourages and directs the daydreaming, many people start to experience pseudoreincarnation memories. The results are just as illusory as those obtained under hypnosis. There are also people who claim to be able to read the past lives of anyone else. This is a specialised use of ordinary psychic perception and it is discussed in detail in Chapter Eight. For the moment let me say that I have known several past-life readers whose impressions I believe were entirely imaginary. Anyone can spin stories about your so-called past life. How on earth are you going to tell whether it is true or not?

Next on our list of courses that do not work is astral projection. Again this is not because the phenomenon does not occur — astral projection really does take place. The illusion lies in most of the systems that claim to teach you how to do it. Astral projection is also known as astral travel — it is the experience of finding yourself outside of your physical body. It is definitely not a dream. A person who is astral travelling is as awake as you are now. Reports of people who have done it while under an anaesthetic in hospital are common. There are also many cases of people who have experienced it when rendered unconscious by an accident. A few people have found themselves outside their body when in the process of falling asleep. Naturally, in the latter case, one might think it is just a dream. To anyone who has had the experience this is obviously not correct. Dreaming and astral projection have nothing in common. However, there are credulous people who do consider every vivid dream to be an astral projection. Some even claim that everyone automatically astral travels when asleep. No-one who has experienced a genuine astral projection could make such a false statement.

This phenomenon is not particularly rare. I have met many people who have had the experience and have had it myself. However, most people will encounter it only once or twice in a lifetime. A tiny minority has astral projections several times, some even a few times a year. Occult books and occult teachers claim that anyone can learn to do it. Lobsang Rampa, who claimed to be a Tibetan lama though he neither spoke nor wrote Tibetan, wrote that all you have to do is lie on your back and imagine yourself floating upwards. Alas, this is not so. There are processes by which you can learn to imagine yourself very vividly somewhere else. Today several parapsychologists are experimenting with such imagination under the name "distant viewing". A few people with psychic perception have been able to describe events many kilometres away. This is not astral travel either. Still others use hypnotism to create an impression of being elsewhere. None of these processes is genuine astral projection.

A few people who have regular astral experiences have written books about them. The best is by Sylvan Muldoon and Hereward Carrington, *The Projection of the Astral Body*. Muldoon found himself slipping out of his body regularly and set up a series of experiments to discover what conditions made it more likely to occur. Eventually he reached the point where he could induce a projection whenever he applied himself to a few days of steady effort. Several of my friends have experimented with the exercises Muldoon set out. Most people have given up after a time but one or two have succeeded in inducing at least one astral projection. None of them has managed to achieve astral travel at will, and I have not met anyone who could. Most purported teachers of astral travel merely exploit the imagination of their more gullible students. A common method is simply to encourage the student to imagine himself or herself somewhere else and then to assure him or her that he or she has astral travelled to that

place. Other courses are built up of lectures and instructions but
then the student is expected to do the actual practical work on his
or her own. Naturally not many of them succeed in doing so.

Another ploy is to encourage students to discuss their dreams.
Studying your own dreams will tend to make those dreams
become more vivid. In no time at all some students will be
convinced that their dreams are astral projection. There are even
con men who promise to give you lessons while you sleep. They
will visit you on the astral plane to help you in your progress.
This is the most blatant fraud imaginable since the trickster does
nothing but take your money. In nineteenth-century America
fraudulent Spiritualism was big business. "Lessons while you
sleep" were available from several dubious teachers. They
included psychic development and contact with the spirit world
as well as astral projection. Fortunately nowadays this
elementary fraud is not so common. A variation on it is used by
certain organisations that have a "spiritual master" at the head.
He or she is supposed to psychically oversee the progress of all
who join the group. There will always be a few disciples who
swear the master has helped their lives, directed their actions or
imparted psychic skills, all from the astral plane.

During my years of investigating Spiritualism I have come
across only one case of deliberate fraud. This was a famous
British medium who pulled faces in a dark room and claimed the
faces belonged to the spirits of the dead. Friends of mine have
encountered two more, both mediums who produced trinkets
purported to have come from the spirit world. One hid the objects
in the battery compartment of his tape-recorder; the other had
them in her pocket. There are written accounts of fraud among
modern Spiritualists. The most notable is *The Psychic Mafia* by
Keene and Spraggett, which deals with organised fraud in some
Spiritualist holiday camps. These cases are few in number after
more than 10 years of investigation on my part. However, it is
worth taking a look at some of the faking techniques used by
these psychic con artists.

There have always been rumours about psychics who keep
notes on every client. These are then supposedly made available
to other pseudopsychics. A person who visits one psychic will
then have notes about himself or herself passed on to other fakes.
Since many people do traipse from one psychic to another this
would appear to be an obvious ploy. In practice, however, this
technique is rarely used — it is simply too much trouble. Only a
very conscientious, organised and fraudulent reader would use it.
Such a reader is unlikely to be in cooperation with anyone else as
con men are notoriously suspicious of one another. In their book

Keene and Spraggett say that Spiritualist camps spread across America keep files of this sort. During the 1950s and 1960s there were several exposures of fraud in those camps. The late Arthur Ford, long regarded as a genuine medium, was found after his death to have kept a large cache of notes on people.

Any psychic who asks you to write questions on a piece of paper or on a slate is undoubtedly a fraud. There are literally dozens of ways of finding out what you have written, all of them so slick you would never notice. One method is to exchange your paper for another, then enabling yours to be read. Another is to render the envelope transparent with alcohol or by shining a light through it. Yet another method is to have you write on a clipboard. When your sheet of paper is removed an impression of the writing remains, though you would rarely notice this.

Other fakes use a little detective work to uncover facts about you. Women may have their handbags surreptitiously searched. Some fakes go to the trouble of having your house watched. The average fortune-teller would hardly bother to do such a thing, but pseudopsychics who charge hundreds, even thousands of dollars for a reading would find it worthwhile. Similarly the Spiritualist practice of "billet reading" is always fraudulent. Members of the congregation are asked to write questions to the spirits on slips of paper and then the medium answers them without opening the slips. Sometimes he or she does it without even touching them. There has rarely been a genuine case of billet reading but there are still Spiritualist churches where this fraud is practised. Some sincere churches unknowingly allow a fraudulent billet reader to perform on their platform. I first became suspicious of Arthur Ford when I heard of his success in billet reading, and this was long before the discovery of the files in his basement.

Outright fraud among psychic readers is more common in some places than in others. Britain and Australasia are relatively free from it, but North America is infested with so-called "gypsies" who pretend to be psychic in order to fleece the public. Many of them are not really of the gypsy race. These are the ones who like to discover "curses" on unsuspecting clients and then demand huge sums of money to remove the curse. They appear to prey predominantly upon southern and central European immigrants whose cultures still retain belief in witchcraft and evil magic. A common gypsy trick is to tell a married woman that her husband is going to die. Alarmed, the woman races to another gypsy reader who only confirms the reading. However, the reader will probably offer to sell the woman a charm to ward off the death, at a considerable price. The terrified woman soon speeds off in the direction of her bank to get the money. In the 1700s, particularly in France, fortune-tellers would help send a husband to his grave. If a female client seemed pleased when told of her husband's imminent death, the fortune-teller would sell her poison instead of a charm!

The black community in the United States is also afflicted with pseudopsychics of this sort. They usually go by the title of "Sister" or "Mother" and credit themselves with being holy women sent by God to help those in need. At one time several of these people living in Texas advertised as far afield as the Canadian city of Toronto. They offered to provide psychic advice via long-distance telephone calls. I spoke to a reporter who had called one of them as part of a newspaper investigation. A barrage of words had greeted her as soon as the phone was answered: "Honey, I can tell you so much just from the sound of your voice. God loves you, honey lamb, but I sense evil people around you who wish you harm. They is jealous and send bad thoughts towards you. Just send me $90 and I will light a candle for you and pray and call you right back with their name and who they are . . ." Needless to say the reporter did not part with her $90. Instead she reversed the charges on the phone call.

Long-distance readings, particularly by mail, provide a fruitful field for the fake psychic. In England I answered an advertisement for a psychic who offered a year's predictions plus a host of psychic impressions. His charge was low enough to be attractive. Before long I received a packet containing several pages. One set was a typed character analysis. Another couple of pages contained hand-written predictions. Others dealt with general life trends. However, careful examination showed that every one of them was printed — only my name had been added to each page to make it appear personal. The character reading was a standard astrological one for my star sign, Aries. This enterprising advertiser was sending the same packet to everyone who applied.

Another postal advertiser, this time in Australia, offers to answer six questions for the low fee of $10. He claims to be a world-famous psychic and uses the logo, "Nothing hidden from this uncanny man". His technique is to answer all questions using simple commonsense. For example, in reply to: "Will I get well?" he answers, "Yes, if you follow your doctor's advice, eat sensibly and get plenty of exercise". To the question: "Will my business prosper?" he says, "Your business will prosper if you apply yourself to it steadily and work hard". This man is quite harmless and makes no attempt to extort additional money from people. The deception lies in his claim of being clairvoyant. There is an element of humour in some of his answers. In reply to my question: "Will I be living in Sydney or Brisbane?" the uncanny man from whom nothing is hidden replied testily, "I'm not going to answer this as you should know yourself where you are going to live''.

I once knew a fake astrologer who worked a postal business. He was a good showman and gave sun-sign predictions on radio as well as running an astrology column in a local paper. Our town's Astrological Society refused to have anything to do with him as it was well known that he could not even cast a horoscope. He worked out of a small office above a newsagent. When postal applications for horoscopes came in he would pop downstairs to the newsagent to buy a monthly guide to the stars. From this he would copy out by hand the appropriate predictions and send them off to the client as a personally calculated $100 horoscope.

Another astrologer runs a column in one of those free newspapers given away in the inner city. He is not exactly a fake but he has a nasty technique for getting money out of people. He advertises widely. When people ring up he quotes a price of several hundred dollars after demanding their telephone number. Naturally most people decline to engage him at that price. Undaunted, he calls them back to get their birth data ''for research purposes''. Then he phones them several more times for additional information. In this way he soon intimidates large numbers of them into accepting his services.

In India I encountered a distinguished old gentleman who used a similar technique. With his beard and turban he looked most impressive, sitting on a stool at the roadside like some ancient oracle. If anyone approached to inquire how much he charged he would proudly say, ''That is up to you. You pay me only what you think it is worth after I have read for you.'' His readings generally lasted 15 minutes and were the usual mixture of flattery and generalisations. When he had finished he would boldly demand a huge sum of money from the astonished client. Most tourists were unwilling to resist this fierce, bearded gentleman and they soon paid up.

Yet another postal fraud was used by an English palmist. This man really believed in palmistry but was just not very good at it. He ran courses and gave private lessons to students and he also supposedly wrote palmistry articles for a magazine. In fact it was widely known that these were written by a friendly amateur palmist in return for other favours. When people wrote and asked this man for a postal reading he would give their hand prints to one of his students. This unsuspecting person was told to write a full report as an exercise. The palmist then sent the work off to the postal client as his own work, which had the double advantage of keeping the students busy and saving the palmist time and trouble.

These tricks sound easy to detect. We all like to think we are too clever to be duped by a con man. In fact every human being is capable of being fooled and very few of us are really as perceptive as we think. The British Psychical Research Society once held a series of fake seances to determine just how observant people really are. Some of the sitters were warned in advance to be on the lookout for fraud; even so, they failed to detect it. They reported things that had not occurred, failed to notice such events as another person entering the room and they missed obvious clues like a cord running from one piece of furniture to another. Not one of them detected a single trick used by the fake medium.

It is a sad fact that hardly anyone is good at observing mistakes and deceptions. We all tend to trust our own judgement, but all too often that judgement is based on what we want to believe or what we have been led to expect. Consider the following report which was distributed by the AAP news service on 2 May 1984:

> A British doctor who stunned nuns when he walked away from a wheelchair after being blessed by the Pope has confessed it was all a mistake. Dr Jan Lavric told reporters he had been helping to organise a trip for disabled people to meet Pope John Paul II. 'I was tired and sat down in an empty wheelchair,' said Dr Lavric. 'Suddenly a nun wheeled me off and, before I could explain, the Pope had blessed me. I was so embarrassed, I kept quiet. But when I jumped out of the chair, the nuns started shouting, "It's a miracle!"'.'

Sounds silly, doesn't it? But in fact, like those nuns, we all tend to jump to conclusions. The easiest mistake to make is to believe that you will not make any mistakes. A wise plan is to do your best but to remind yourself that you may still be wrong.

Many people have had the experience of odd occurrences around the house. Often an object will disappear, only to reappear some time later. This sort of thing is particularly prone to occur during an outbreak of poltergeist activity. A few people find it happens regularly whether or not there is any other poltergeist activity. How do you tell whether it is a real psychic experience? Here are two cases to illustrate.

I once lived alone in a place where objects tended to vanish. At the time I was doing a lot of work with special white ink which came in small bottles. I kept a bottle on a particular shelf and one day, when I reached up for it, I found it had gone. I was quite sure it had been there so this seemed like a good opportunity to test if my disappearing/reappearing objects were a genuine pheno-menon. From that day I put nothing else on that shelf. Every day I would reach up and check the shelf — this was to confirm that it was really empty. About six weeks into the exercise I reached up and there was the bottle again.

What does this prove? My opinion is that I had proved that disappearance/reappearance really took place. Strictly speaking, however, there are other explanations. Perhaps I had found the bottle myself and absent-mindedly put it back on the shelf. Maybe someone had come into the flat without my knowing and put the bottle on the shelf. These theories are far-fetched but not impossible.

Several years later I was living in a house in Canada with my wife, daughter and young sister-in-law. One day my appointment book, which contained all the details of my business life, vanished from my desk. I had been at the desk answering a phone call at 9 a.m. and writing in the book. Then I had gone upstairs to talk to my wife. When I returned the book was gone. The previous evening I had been carrying out some psychic experiments. It now looked very much as if these experiments had backfired and caused the disappearance of a very important book. We searched high and low, practically taking the house apart piece by piece. Every cupboard, every drawer, every bit of furniture and carpeting was thoroughly searched. That book was gone. I offered a $20 reward to our daughter and teenaged sister-in-law if they could find it. They tried and failed. I offered the same reward to every visitor who called. They all searched the premises with equal lack of success.

If ever a disappearance was proved genuine, this was it. But 10 days later our niece spent the weekend with us. After returning home on the Sunday night we received a phone call from her claiming the reward money. She had found the book! It was in a parcel of books that my wife had given to her.

What had happened was this: I had carried the book from my desk with me upstairs to speak with my wife. During our conversation I had laid it down. Meanwhile my wife was busily piling up our daughter's outgrown books and inadvertently placed these on top of my appointment book. Later she had taken the books to our basement and placed them in a green plastic bag, awaiting the next visit of our niece. During our search of the house it had not occurred to anyone that a green garbage bag in the basement could possibly hold the missing book! Yet it did.

Poor observation, wrong conclusions, mistaken belief; these are a constant danger to the psychic researcher. Perhaps the widest field in which these faults flourish is that of psychic healing. It is another of the subjects often taught to aspiring clairvoyants by teachers with little or no real knowledge. Psychic healing is difficult to assess objectively. All the healers I have met have been completely sincere, but less than five per cent of them struck me as having a genuine healing gift. Psychic healers are

generally honest, well intentioned and lacking in psychic ability.
The typical psychic healer starts by having you sit comfortably or
lie down. He or she will then place his or her hands on your head
or pass them gently up and down your body. Most healers enter a
state of prayer or meditation while they are working. A few pass
into trance. The procedure can last anything from a few seconds
to a couple of hours; twenty minutes is the average. Most healers
ask you to return for further treatments unless your complaint is
minor, such as a headache.

Spiritualist healers consider that the healing power comes from
God or some high spirit. The healer acts merely as a channel. The
occasional independent healer will maintain that the power is
entirely his or her own, a special talent he or she possesses. It is
the easiest psychic talent to convince yourself you have. This is
one reason psychic groups are filled with healers. Another reason
is that healing appeals to people's altruistic tendencies and most
religions attract altruistic people. Many churches and all
Spiritualist groups practise healing. A third reason is that healing
grants social status, and this is particularly appealing to people
who lack other abilities.

My own experience is that people who really do have a healing
gift are usually heavy-set, earthy folk. They tend to have broad
hands like those of a farmer. By contrast the vast tribes of
pseudohealers are usually slim, fine-boned, sensitive people.
Nothing will convince these pseudohealers that they do not have
the gift. Why does this illusion persist? In the first place, people
who go to a healer love the attention: it is undeniably pleasant to
have someone touching you in a caring way. This means that all
patients respond favourably to a psychic healer regardless of his or
her actual ability. No-one is going to be so unfeeling as to rise
from the couch and announce that the whole exercise is a fraud.
Then, too, most people who come for healing suffer from
relatively minor complaints. Others have painful yet essentially
harmless ailments like rheumatism. These medical problems
seldom get much better or much worse. The patient rarely has
cause to declare the healer a failure as most illnesses disappear
naturally. The few that do not will result in the patient going to
hospital and thus being out of the psychic healer's keeping. Since
patients with serious complaints are likely to seek orthodox
treatment as well as psychic healing, there is every chance they
will get better whether the healer helps or not.

Patients with terminal complaints sometimes seek a healer
before they die. Their death is never counted as a failure: one
reason is that healers do not claim to cure the terminally ill; and
another is that the patient is believed to have been "helped" even

though he or she died in the end. In short, psychic healing is a no-lose situation. No wonder there is such a plethora of it. A healer who is sympathetic and understanding is bound to attract clients. These in turn attract others, since people assume that a busy healer is a successful one. People are more likely to attribute their eventual recovery to a healer who has a good reputation and so his or her circle of clients grows.

It is a curious fact that in Spiritualist groups people who come for healing often take up healing themselves. Healing groups breed new healers. Finally there is a lot to be said for the old concept of faith-healing. When a client believes in the doctor, the priest or the shaman, his or her own belief may well hasten a cure. Fortunately the whole business is pretty harmless. For that reason I have no quarrel with the psychic healers, alleged or real. Indeed, since they all offer help and support to those in need, they are to be commended. Furthermore there is always the chance of a genuine psychic healing. Miracles have happened under the most unlikely circumstances. Among the hosts of healers there are undoubtedly some who do possess a special gift. It would be a rash person who would go among them declaring who was fit and who was self-deluded. The game changes, however, when a healer decides to charge money. In churches, Spiritualist and otherwise, healing is available for no charge. Many freelance healers practise for nothing but some do charge. There is no reason why even a pseudohealer should not be paid for his or her time and trouble, but why pay for something when it is freely available elsewhere? The payment of fees brings the danger of charlatans entering the field. High charges for fake cures are usually the province of fraudulent "doctors". Every year sees a new cancer quack setting up to extort money from desperate people. Psychic healers are rarely caught in such a fraud, though there are exceptions.

The one place where fake psychic healing is endemic is in the Philippines. The infamous psychic surgeons of this country have been exposed many times, yet still people flock to them. Americans regularly fly out to undergo fake surgical operations. The conjuring tricks used by these Filipinos are slick and the average person has no hope of uncovering them. Thousands of dollars are taken in regularly by these psychic tricksters.

My advice to the reader is to give psychic healing a complete miss. It has no connection with true psychic development. Why waste your time on something which is at best a sidetrack and only one more of the many false trails? If you must dabble at least try to set up some tests. You should also endeavour to gain as much medical knowledge as you can. To become a doctor requires many years of training. Good doctors then spend the rest of their lives keeping up with the latest medical advances. The typical psychic healer sets up without the slightest knowledge of anatomy, physiology, disease or anything else. He or she lacks the most elementary understanding of the workings of the body or the symptoms of disease. Since the activities are doing no harm this ignorance makes little difference. But what happens when a seriously ill person arrives for treatment? If the healer does not know what is wrong there is a real danger the patient may fail to call in orthodox medical aid. Every healer should at least be able to recognise a serious ailment.

Setting up a test of healing ability is not easy. Parapsychologists who have studied the problem have come up with techniques that are too difficult for the backyard investigator — some involve laboratory mice or flasks of cell tissues. However, you can make a point of keeping careful records of your healing activities. These should include a detailed description of the condition before treatment and progress reports as the healing continues. This will not establish whether or not you have psychic healing ability, but it will enable you to find out if you are getting results.

You might try only pretending to give someone a treatment. Then see if the patient reacts differently to the real thing. If you ever come across a group of animals or even plants that have a common disease, you could try healing one half of them and then compare your results with the other half. Another possibility would be to work on minor illnesses that have a known recovery time. The common cold or sore throat are good examples. If you can speed up the recovery time you will have demonstrated something, but even this may be suggestion rather than psychic power. For those who feel they have the gift of "absent healing", that is, healing someone from a distance without direct contact, you could attempt to heal a person's cold without telling him or her. If the cold suddenly disappears you may be really onto something.

This chapter may seem depressing with its endless lists of false paths. Cheer up! There are plenty of things you can do with genuine psychic ability. Psychic research would not be so interesting if there were not both truth and falsehood along the way.

Chapter Eight
SOME SPECIAL PSYCHIC TECHNIQUES

Do you believe in ghosts or hauntings? I do because I have experienced them. Quite early in my psychic career I spent some time in a haunted building. There were ghostly footsteps, self-opening doors, blasts of ice-cold electrified air and a disembodied voice. To a young psychical researcher it seemed a heaven-sent chance for investigation. I have encountered four more hauntings since my first experience and was able to check out all of them. Several of my friends and acquaintances have also encountered hauntings.

It does not take any special psychic power to deal with a haunting. Any prolonged involvement with psychic matters will inevitably provide this phenomenon. It helps to know what to do. My own first encounter occurred in a haunted army hospital where I worked during my years of national service. It was not actually a full-scale hospital but merely the regimental medical post. We had three hospital beds but spent most of our time on simple first aid and the dispensing of medicine. It was rare for sick soldiers to be in the hospital after dark.

There were two other medics besides myself. We would take turns sleeping in the place while the others slept in the barracks a kilometre away. It did not take us long to discover that the place was haunted. Footsteps would sound along the corridor through the night, and our front door regularly opened and closed itself as the footsteps came in or out. A column of cold air could be felt moving round with the footsteps. Many people felt the hair on the back of their necks stand up when this presence was in the building. An electric shock seemed to pass through the air — visitors described it as a creepy or scary sensation. Any medic asleep in the building could be awakened by ghostly fingers playing over his face. There would be the sense of someone leaning over him accompanied by the familiar electric shock. Several soldiers confided in us that they were afraid to go near the place after dark.

By coincidence the other two medics who worked with me were also interested in psychical matters. We were thoroughly frightened, but at the same time fascinated by what we were experiencing so intensely. Of course these phenomena are the traditional ones associated with a haunting; there is nothing remarkable about them. At the time we had no idea what was causing them. Later I learned that a young soldier had died in the building only two years before from an undiagnosed brain tumour.

After several weeks we rang up some local Spiritualists. They sensibly cautioned us to first ensure there was not an animal or other natural explanation for what was going on. They then advised us to talk to the spirit and tell it to go away. We were to explain that if it looked around, it would find other spirits to guide it to its proper place. Feeling rather foolish, we held a small ceremony to do as we had been instructed. To our utter amazement it worked. The phenomena ceased completely. We were actually disappointed at the loss of our ghostly companion.

But was it really a ghost? Some time later I read the book *Real Magic* by Isaac Bonewits. This is one of the best books ever written on magical practices. Bonewits proposed that a haunting is not really a disembodied spirit but rather a sort of recording of something that has happened in the past. In support of this he points out that any type of exorcism will serve to halt a haunting; Roman Catholic exorcisms, Spiritualist exorcisms, pagan exorcisms — they all work equally well. Our particular technique of talking to the supposed spirit is no better or worse than any other method. While I talked to the spirit my two companions swore they could hear a whisper which seemed to answer my words. Certainly the thing behaved as if it were a spirit. But there is no positive proof that it was.

For anyone who encounters a haunting I recommend the following method for dealing with it:

1. Set aside a special time for the attempt at exorcism. It will probably be at night since most manifestations are stronger after dark. There is often a particular hour at which the ghost is most likely to appear.
2. Conduct a small cleansing ritual. A good method is to sprinkle a few drops of water in every room or to light a few candles. Perhaps you might like to offer a prayer or a few words in each room.
3. Address yourself to the empty air as if the spirit were there before you. Tell it that it does not belong here. Advise it to move on to its own place. Tell it to look around for other spirits who will act as guides. Inform the spirit that you wish it no harm but that it must not stay.

You may feel pretty idiotic doing this but, believe me, it works. Your haunting will cease forthwith. Most people who encounter a haunting are scared stiff. There is a reason for this and it is not merely a fear of the unknown. All hauntings carry with them a curious creepy sensation, often like a cloud of evil or depression. Naturally people assume they are dealing with an evil spirit, but there is nothing evil about it. This is merely the way a haunting manifests. I have encountered this sensation many times and am never scared by it now. However, it can certainly be terrifying the first time you meet it.

Besides actual hauntings, many buildings possess an atmosphere. Some are so strong that everyone who enters notices it. The most obvious examples are old churches, particularly cathedrals. There the feeling of peace and devotion is so prominent that even a cynical atheist will notice it. My years of psychic work have taught me that it is possible to deliberately create an atmosphere in a building. It is also possible to remove a negative feeling. These are things that cannot be proved scientifically. I have cautioned you to take nothing on trust, to test everything you read. But with atmospheres, you will simply have to rely on your own judgement.

One case cropped up which did seem to offer objective evidence. When I was 17 I stayed for a week in a university residential college. Fellow students informed me that my room had never been occupied for any length of time. Years before someone had hung himself in that room and since then no-one had stayed in it for long. I lasted seven days and then left the college for personal reasons. The room itself had nothing to do with my leaving. However, I have often wondered if it did have some subconscious effect upon me. Certainly there was no haunting in that room; yet if it could be shown that students vacated it far more frequently than any other room, this would be objective evidence of some special factor at work.

The method for clearing a bad atmosphere from a place is similar to that for getting rid of a haunting. Simply enter every room and carry out a simple symbolic action to clear it. I did this once with a 'friend whose new home was thoroughly gloomy. I walked through every room splashing drops of water out of a bowl. Within days the gloom had lifted and left no trace. Another friend bought a house that had been owned by schizophrenics. She and her children felt the need for a cleansing of the place so they made up a tray of fruit and sweets. This was carried solemnly through every room, set down for a few minutes and the room was blessed. No scientist would agree that such an action could have any effect. But she and the children were more than satisfied with the results.

The technique for putting a new atmosphere into a place is not so easy. If you want to turn your house into a centre of happiness there are no short cuts. You will have to spend time there, doing enjoyable things and thinking happy thoughts. At the same time you have to concentrate on driving these emotions into the very walls of your home. Does this sound fanciful? Try it sometime. I do this regularly with every house or office I have. Within a month or two visitors invariably comment, "Oh, what a good feeling this place has! I felt comfortable as soon as I stepped inside." Can these reactions really be due to chance?

Objects sometimes have an atmosphere or an aura around them. My experience with such things is limited, but there are hundreds of stories of this phenomenon. Once you have developed psychic perception you can pick up impressions from any object. Those with an aura so strong that anyone can detect it are quite rare. You read in Chapter Three about the barber's chair whose owner had died of cancer. My father had an anecdote of a similar nature. His grandparents lived in India and brought back various curios to their home in England. When Dad was a young man a visitor with psychic perception called at the house. She immediately declared that there was something abominable in the house. This visitor prowled from room to room, eventually making her way to the attic. Here she opened a trunk and drew out an antique knife. This, she declared, was the abominable object. My father made inquiries and found that it was a ceremonial harem knife, used for executing any harem woman who was unfaithful. When I asked him what had become of the knife, he sat silent for a few minutes. Then he said, "I took it with me to the Isle of Man. Halfway across, I dropped it into the sea!"

There is a theory that mechanical devices are more likely to pick up an aura from their owner than other objects. For example, there are many stories about clocks that stopped or started at the precise moment of their owners' deaths. Psychical researcher Elliott O'Donnell made a special collection of such cases in the pages of the *Occult Review*. Hereward Carrington also collected similar stories. In the same way many a person fond of his or her car has found it to behave quite differently in the hands of a stranger. I have known two people with old cars that ran perfectly, only to break down irreparably once sold to someone else. Secretaries who use electric typewriters have told me they can tell if someone else has used their machine. Computer-terminal operators have made similar claims. You probably know at least one person who finds that watches, tape-recorders and other electrical devices tend to malfunction in his or her presence. In all these cases it seems that the mechanical object is somehow picking up something from the owner. No doubt this is the same sort of "something" which builds up the atmosphere in a building.

Some years ago I devised an experiment dealing with the impression of thought into an object. A friend had sent me a little brass Buddha from Nepal. I decided to use it as a test object. Whenever I had any psychic work to do or whenever I practised meditation, I would keep the brass Buddha beside me. I would hold it in my hands whenever any psychic or spiritual exercise was taking place. The intention was to imbue it with the thought that it was a psychic or spiritual instrument. After two years I took it to a class of people studying psychometry. Every one of them declared that it felt like a source of power; some likened it to an electric battery. Since then I have tried it on several other people who claim psychic ability, always with the same result.

In Chapter Three I mentioned the use of psychometry to trace the history of ancient objects. This is another fascinating extension of the psychic sense but, like the others, it is fraught with danger. The term "psychic archaeology" has been used for this practice. A recent book, *The Psychic Detectives*, by Colin Wilson summarises much of what has been done in this field. The first major study of psychometry for archaeological purposes was *The Soul of Things* by William Denton, published in 1873. Denton got psychometrists to study artefacts from ancient Rome and Greece and also certain mineral specimens. His three-volume book on the subject records uncanny successes with psychics giving accurate accounts of life in ancient cities. Unfortunately the same book includes psychic perceptions of other planets which proved to be totally mistaken. The problem is that imagination tends to intrude unless close checks are kept on the psychic.

As a general rule, never try any psychic perception unless there is a way to prove whether it is true or not. Uncontrolled imagination is the great enemy. You must be constantly on your guard. Some of the practices in this chapter verge on magic rather than psychic perception. Once you have developed your psychic sense it is natural to ask: "Can it be used for influencing things, rather than just perceiving them?" The answer would seem to be yes. I have met many people who dabble in magic. They include followers of witchcraft, ceremonial magic, natural magic and the native magical practices of Africa, Australia and the West Indies. My conclusion is that 95 per cent of it is no more than a game. Casting spells, carrying out rituals and holding ceremonies may be fun but it has precious little effect. I have known nearly a dozen covens of witches and not one of them could achieve any results. As a matter of fact none of them had any ESP either. Mind you, most of the "high priests" and "high priestesses" played around with tarot cards and considered themselves to be psychic. However, this still leaves that five per cent who dabble in magic and do get results. Let us take a look at them.

The best name for this special success factor is "the magical state of mind". It is very similar to the state of mind required for exercising ESP. I have no doubt the two are related. In most tribal societies medicine men or the equivalent are selected when quite young. They are picked for their natural talent for the work. Out of a dozen young men who show an interest, perhaps one or two will show some natural ability. Similarly, in ordinary western society there is a smattering of people who regularly produce magical results. Few of them are members of occult societies and one can find them anywhere.

A typical example is my friend Harry Reimesmar, mentioned in Chapter Five. He is the man who can influence a pack of cards when someone else is shuffling them. Perhaps the most success-ful magician I know is Peter Macey, a 35-year-old electrician. He casts no spells, but Peter has complete faith in his ability to make things happen. Almost invariably they do. When Peter needs a parking spot for his car, there it is. When Peter wants a particular item, no matter how obscure, it turns up at a discount sale within days. When Peter needs to see a particular person, there is a knock on his door. In fact there is virtually nothing that does not happen when Peter decides it should. Peter has two characteristics which play a part in this. In the first place, he is hyperactive so that his life is filled with activity even without the magical talent. Secondly, he has developed his psychic perception very much as explained in this book. The combination of good ESP and plenty of activity seems to result in successful magic. I think that our old friend, the believing–doubting tightrope, is at work here. The "belief" is faith that the magic will work. The "doubt" ensures that you do everything practical to bring things about rather than waiting for the magic. You have to believe in your ability but you have to get on with things in a perfectly normal way as if you did not believe at all. As the saying goes, "Heaven helps those who help themselves".

My advice is to decide what you want to happen and then to do everything you can to bring it about. While doing so, keep in mind that you are practising magic. Believe in your own magical ability. At first this attitude may make no difference. After a time, if you persist, you will get results which go beyond what you could reasonably expect. You will have achieved a magical state of mind and magic will work for you. I have learned to do this. So have others who developed their ESP as shown in this book. All the people I know who possess the magical state of mind make free use of psychic perception. There is little doubt that the two things, magic and ESP, are linked. Try it yourself.

Very few of the folk I know who play around with witchcraft and other forms of magic really get results. The few who do have two things in common: they have a good opinion of themselves along with faith in their magical ability; and secondly, they are also distinctly cynical. They have no faith in the claims of other people or in rules laid down in the various occult books. In short, they are walking the believing–doubting tightrope. Most people who can make things happen specialise in one or two effects. It is a rare person like Peter who gets results in many different fields.

For example, I have a magical knack for finding out-of-print books. Not only do rare books turn up wherever I look for them, but also I have frequently made up my mind to find a particular volume and had that book in my hands within a month. This particular magical knack is not uncommon with collectors. I have met others who can do the same. Researchers who hunt out information in libraries and newspaper files sometimes develop a gift for finding just what they need. Many writers report the same phenomenon.

Then there are those who have an affinity for money. Everything they do turns to gold. Other folk, working in similar conditions, plod along with just enough money to get them by. Many of those who attract money put it down to good judgement. Others admit that they do have a magical knack for it. Some people have an affinity for plants, machinery or animals. Next time you meet such a person, discuss what I have named "the magical state of mind". I am sure your will find them interested.

It may well be that ESP actually makes magic easier. Perhaps the psychic perception simply helps you to find the right opportunities. It results in you being at the right place at the right time. In Chapter Six I discussed my views on the nature of time and the current of events which constitute time itself. Another way of looking at this is to say that ESP helps you to tune into the most beneficial of the time currents to achieve what you want. Whatever the explanation, the "magical state of mind" is an obvious next step for anyone wanting to develop their psychic abilities.

Psychic perception can be useful in many different ways. Unfortunately not all of them can be objectively tested to prove that they exist. For example, once your ESP is working there is nothing to stop you from reaching out to the consciousness of animals or even plants. Does this sound like a far-fetched idea? Perhaps it is. Certainly it is hard to prove you really can talk to the trees or prattle to your poodle on a telepathic wavelength. But you can have a lot of fun trying! However, the great danger with these sorts of exercises is that imagination will take over. This cannot be stressed too often. Therefore I advise you never to try these things before you are thoroughly experienced with ordinary ESP, which can be checked and tested objectively.

Talking to trees is a simple process. Just put your hand on the tree trunk and clear your mind. You will find that impressions come flowing in almost immediately. Unlike the impressions you get from a ring or a watch, these really appear to be the thoughts and feelings of the tree itself. Feelings are more common than thoughts. Many trees react with a feeling of curiosity ("Who are you?") as soon as they become aware of your presence. Other trees radiate a feeling of affection. To me it seems as though they are asking for a cuddle. A number of times I have found myself putting my arms around a trunk to hug it, much to the surprise of anyone who happens to be in the vicinity. I have also found plants that are distinctly antagonistic towards humans. Trees can hardly be said to think but they do have an awareness of things around them and they do have wants. Touching a tree will sometimes let you see the surrounding landscape from that tree's point of view. Trees in well-frequented public parks often give a picture of the park as it has existed over many years. A tree's awareness is very much slower than that of an animal — their perceptions and thoughts are measured in days rather than minutes. Most trees are more awake during the night. Doubtless this is because they draw in most nourishment at this time. In the hottest part of the day a tree may be almost asleep.

There are two ways of testing these things, both of which I have used myself. The first is to close your eyes and have someone take you round to various trees. Ask them to take you to the trees that give the strongest impressions more than once, but without telling you which is which. If you can record the same reaction each time from the same tree, you have some evidence. The first time I did this exercise there were two interesting occurrences. A clump of thin bushes gave the impression of being a sort of group entity, many voices, but all bound together. Every time my friend led me near them I sensed this, so that I was able to tell him whenever we neared that corner of the park. One particular tree gave a curious sensation of pride and isolation: "I am the lord of the park", it seemed to say. I encountered this once more and assumed it was the same tree. It was not; it was, however, another tree of the same species.

Another form of testing is simply to have another person with psychic perception talk to the same trees. Naturally you must not compare notes while doing this. Afterwards, if you find that you have both received similar or identical reactions, you will have another piece of evidence. A cynic may see this as just telepathy between two people. This might be so, but it is quite unlikely.

There have been many people who have learned to communicate with plants. Most are discussed in *The Secret Life of Plants*, by Thompkins and Bird. When that book came out all sorts of plant owners started talking to their greenery in an effort to make them grow faster. Perhaps if more people learned to listen to their plants, rather than chatting to them, real communication could be achieved.

Psychic communication with animals is more difficult. Animals, like people, communicate mainly through the senses. When an animal is in your presence its mind is usually too active for ESP to take place. Just as the human mind tends to block out psychic awareness, so, too, does the mind of the animal. So the trick is to reach out to the mind of your cat or dog when it is relaxed and not paying much attention. There have always been stories about psychic animals. The ordinary household pet will sometimes show psychic flashes. But to achieve regular psychic contact with an animal is rare. Furthermore you can use your psychic sense to reach out to an animal mind, but you cannot send your thoughts across to it. Unless your pet decides to tune into you it will be a one-way communication. Fortunately many pets do decide to do just that.

Select a time when your animal is alone and resting. Go up to it quietly so as not to disturb it and sit down. Then try to tune in. Cats and dogs react quite differently: the mind of a cat is completely alien; a dog's mind is much closer to a human one. When probing a cat's mind you will often find it works on two or more levels at the same time. Three quite different mental processes may be going on at once. But when a cat concentrates on something its mind develops a sort of tunnel vision, locking out other thoughts in a way a human can scarcely comprehend. A cat's emotional state can be far more intense and pervasive than any human emotion. Dogs, on the other hand, resemble nothing so much as a child. As the dog ages it gains adult experience and wisdom, but its thoughts and feelings remain very like those of a young human being.

Tuning into animals is a most interesting experience but I have not found it particularly useful. Other people, notably Barbara Woodhouse, renowned British dog-trainer, have found the reverse. She maintains that the human mind can link up with the animal's in a psychic sense. Allen Bond, author of *Kinship with All Life* and *Letters to Strongheart*, attributed his dog's success as a canine film star to a telepathic link with its trainer. Strongheart was a German shepherd who took Hollywood by storm in the 1930s. He starred in a number of movies, including *White Fang*. He was responsible for much of the modern popularity of the

German shepherd breed and his intelligence and natural acting ability were legendary. Bond had established the habit of reading to Strongheart every day. Not only did the dog listen with interest, he quickly showed a preference for certain types of literature. Serious literature fascinated him; light novels and magazines bored him stiff. If Bond neglected the reading Strongheart would pester him until he remembered. There can be no suggestion that the dog really understood every word; rather he was picking up the thoughts behind what Bond read out. I have known many dogs who obviously tried to read their owners' minds. This is in keeping with the dogs' enjoyment of doing things with their owners. Mind you, I have also known plenty of other dogs who never attempted any such thing.

Fascinating as these exercises are, psychic perception is more useful when applied to other human beings. The final technique I want to share with you is probing another person's past incarnations. In Chapter Seven I warned that many techniques of recovering past lives are little more than an illusion. Using your own ESP to look at past lives can be quite illusory as well. Nevertheless, it is well worth making the attempt. The basic technique is merely to sit with someone and tune in to him or her with the intention of uncovering his or her past lives. Naturally you can only do this if you have first learned to tune in in the usual way. Psychometry is the obvious way to start, although you will find that for reincarnation readings it is better to work without holding anything. A personal object makes a good starting point, but is liable to limit you to the present time. Before long you will start to find your mind flooding with impressions. It is wise to have a tape-recorder going while you work as this type of reading gives more information than you can possibly remember. Be aware that there is a constant danger of imagination taking over. There are also several possible sources of error. Here are some cases which illustrate these points:

At a party I offered to work on a small group of people, getting impressions of past lives for each of them. Naturally they were all eager, and most of the others in the room turned their attention to my efforts as well. Starting with a middle-aged man I immediately picked up an adventurous life in the American Wild West, about the middle of last century. This lifetime had little in common with the typical Hollywood western. There had been plenty of hard, dull work, much traipsing from town to town and a lot of time spent out of doors. There were no gunfights or stagecoach hold-ups but there were myriad details about jobs, locales and other matters. One particular point was the fact that the man had made himself his own set of false teeth out of steel.

At the end of my reading the man offered some comments: "What you have been describing is the life of my great-grandfather. We have his diaries at home and everything you have told me is contained in them, even the steel teeth."

I do not believe that this man was the reincarnation of his own ancestor. Obviously what I had tuned into was his own memory of the relative's writings. Scratch this attempt at a past incarnation! Moving on to the next person I again picked up vivid details of a past life. This one was in Edwardian England, judging from the style of the clothes and furnishings. I could see him as a young boy, in a house where he had gone for a holiday. There was a piano that would not play and a doghouse but no dog. A nurse or someone similar was caring for the boy. This man, too, had interesting comments to make on my work: "That's me, all right," he agreed, "but in this lifetime! I was 10 years old at the time you described. I was dressed in old-fashioned clothes, just as you said, but it certainly was not the Edwardian period. It was just 20 years ago."

I do not remember how the other cases went that night, but these two incidents illustrate perfectly how easily one can go wrong. The ESP was spot on, but the information simply was not what it had seemed to be. So even if your psychic impressions are true, there is no guarantee that they are a genuine reincarnation memory. There is a distinct probability that they will not be. Here are two further cases. I was once reading for a man I knew only slightly but in company with a friend who knew him well. Three distinct incarnations came through, plus fragments of others. One life was as a farm labourer, another as a horseback courier while a third was the life of a settler in the Australian outback. There was no way of confirming that any one of these impressions was true. My friend, however, afterward told me this: "Do you realise that in all of those lives you described he was living alone? As long as I've known him, he's been a loner. Those lives sound just like the way he is now."

Two explanations are possible, apart from simple coincidence. The first is that these incarnations were genuine. Several lives in solitary circumstances had led to this man's present personality as a loner. The other is that these lives were merely dramatisations of his current personality. They had been conjured up by my psychic perception of his character. Of the two, I think the second one is more likely.

On another occasion I detected several incarnations for a young woman. One of these was set in Britain after the withdrawal of the Roman legions. During that life she had had a habit of getting up at dawn to greet the sun with upraised arms. "But that's exactly what I do now!'' she exclaimed. ''Ever since I was a little girl, I've done that. I don't know how I came to start but somehow it just seemed the right thing to do.'' Was this habit an echo of something she did in a previous life? That would explain such a curious ritual. Or had I merely picked something out of her present life and interpreted it as a past incarnation? There is really no way of learning the truth.

My advice is that you experiment with this technique for yourself. Just be sure not to attempt it until you can achieve a high degree of accuracy with ordinary ESP. If you try it before you are thoroughly experienced you will simply encourage your mind to fantasise. As has been said many times, that is a sure way to destroy your psychic perception. You must keep a record of what you do. Include notes on the comments of the people concerned as to the relevance of what you tell them. But do not let yourself get carried away with such experiments. Fit them in between other, more verifiable exercises. These will help to keep your feet on the ground. One benefit of reincarnation work is that some of what you discover may be of value to the people for whom you read. It often provides psychological clues to help the person sort out current problems or to understand difficult situations. The reading can also give material for discussion. Just be sure you explain to the person that there is no guarantee of the authenticity of the material you get.

There is an interesting psychological exercise which can produce another type of pseudo-reincarnation reading. It is called the Cristos Experience. As with all techniques for recovering past lives, there is reason to doubt that these past lives are genuine. The Cristos Experience is a method of controlled visualisation — it is sometimes described as a waking dream. It produces visions similar to those that can be evoked under hypnosis. Unlike hypnosis, however, the experimenter remains awake and in full control of his or her senses at all times. This special state has actually been known about for a long time — it was one of the secrets of Britain's most famous magical society, the Order of the Golden Dawn — and occultists and magicians had to train hard to achieve it. The Cristos Experience is a modern, simple method of getting the same result. Anyone can do it.

The Cristos Experience became popular in the 1970s through the books of G. M. Glaskin, notably his first volume entitled *Windows of the Mind.* In actual fact the technique had been published in America a decade earlier under the title *Awareness Techniques.* You need two people besides the experimenter. The experimenter starts by lying down comfortably in a quiet place with his (or her) shoes removed. One person then begins to massage the experimenter's ankles. The other person rubs the experimenter's forehead with a closed fist in a circular motion; this is continued for about five minutes. After that the person who massaged the ankles is no longer required but may remain in the room.

Now you ask the experimenter to imagine that his body is growing five centimetres longer from the feet. Most people take a few minutes to imagine this. Ask him to tell you when he has succeeded. Next, tell him to imagine that he has grown another five centimetres, this time upwards from the head. When he has done that ask him to imagine that this time he is stretching 60 centimetres downwards. After this he must grow 60 centimetres longer in an upwards direction. Next instruct him to imagine that his whole body is swelling up like a balloon. He must continue with this exercise till his body is nearly the size of the room. Tell him to imagine he is floating upwards, out through the roof and up into the air.

Now instruct him to imagine that he is at his front door. Make him describe it to you. Get the experimenter to tell you as much detail as he can, such as the colour of the door and any marks or special features. If the person claims he is unable to visualise things, tell him to describe the door from memory. You are unlikely to get any more protests after that. When he has given as much detail as he can, ask him if he notices anything different about the door from the last time he saw it. Next ask him to imagine he is up on the roof, above the door. What can he see? Get him to describe the scene in as much detail as possible. Also ask him to look in different directions so that he has examined the scene from all possible angles. If he tells you that he cannot see or imagine clearly, just get him to continue looking round and reporting whatever he can. When this is done ask him whether it is night or day. Most people will reply that it is daytime, even if the experiment is carried out at night. Ask him to reverse it, to change day to night or vice versa. Tell him to describe the scene under these changed conditions. Then ask him: "Who is it who has changed it from day to night?" Most people will reply, "I did because you asked me to". If he says something else, gently point out the correct answer. Now ask him to imagine he is floating up into the air; get him to float for a long time. When he is ready tell him to float down to the ground. Up to this point the experimenter has simply been using his imagination, but the exercise has encouraged his imagination to become stronger and stronger. He is now at the stage when he is going to pass out of ordinary imagination into the special state of visualisation for which you are aiming.

When he comes down ask him where he is. He may tell you that he finds himself somewhere interesting but most people describe a rather nondescript scene. Many find themselves on a road, a beach, open countryside or somewhere similar. Ask him to walk along in this place and tell you what he sees. Before long he will start to describe all sorts of things. There may be a town or a city, buildings, people or anything else. Many declare that they seem to belong here and that they have somehow taken on a new identity. They may have a career, family, etcetera. Encourage him to describe everything he sees and to examine anything of interest that he comes across.

You will often get good results by asking him to look down at his feet. Almost invariably this leads to the discovery that his appearance has completely changed. His clothes and even his body have metamorphosed. While he is undergoing the Cristos Experience get him to describe everything he sees and does. Take care not to suggest anything to him. This experience is entirely his own and you must not try to influence it in any way. Once or twice during the experiment remind him that he is really lying in the room talking to you — he will readily agree. Even though he is experiencing this dream-like vision, he is always fully aware of his real situation. It has been truly called a waking dream.

All the steps in the Cristos Experience have been carefully set out. You must not deviate from them in any way. The initial massage of head and ankles helps to disorient the experimenter — it upsets his usual body awareness. The stretching exercises are the first steps in imagination and also serve to liberate the experimenter from his usual perception of his own body. The visualisation of the door and later the scene from the roof are both vital steps. The question, "Who is making it night or day?" is a safeguard, designed to remind the person that he is in control of the whole thing. The progressive exploration, when the person first "lands" after floating, deepens and intensifies the experience. Literally everyone who tries the experience reaches the state of the waking dream. What they experience, however, varies from person to person. People are invariably fascinated by the experience since it is unlike anything they have tried before.

It has been claimed that the Cristos Experience recovers past lives. In view of the fact that people have had experiences as elves, fairies and spacemen, this would seem highly unlikely. The truth is that it liberates the dreaming function of the mind while the person is fully awake. It is possible that the experience may contain some paranormal elements. A person who is psychic may indeed tune into the life of another person, past or present. Alternatively his experience may contain fragments of the past or future. But to put the whole thing down as a recall of past lives is downright false. The experience is completely harmless. There is no such thing as losing control, being unable to come out of the experience or finding the experience intrudes into real life at a later date. For anyone interested in psychic matters it is an obvious exercise to try, although strictly speaking there is nothing psychic about it. If nothing else, it will familiarise you with a state of mind which might easily be mistaken for astral travel or past-life regression.

The techniques in this chapter complete all the forms of psychic perception I know of, but there is no reason for you not to delve further. Be alert and critical, adventurous and curious and see just how much more you can uncover.

Chapter Nine
THE HIGHER PATH
OF SPIRITUAL DEVELOPMENT

Have you ever wondered about your own spiritual state? No doubt you have if you are interested in psychic matters. Because of my experience in the psychic field, people often ask me questions about spiritual development. Recently at a party, for example, a thin young man approached me with a question. From his earnest expression and ascetic appearance, I guessed what he wanted even before he spoke.

"I hear you do psychic readings," he began.

"Not professionally," I replied, "but, yes, I have some ESP. What can I do for you?"

"What can you tell me about my spiritual evolution?" he asked.

I have a standard reply to this question and I used it with the young man. "What do you mean by spiritual evolution?"

He looked puzzled. People who ask this question usually do. "Oh, I don't know," he said. "Can't you look at my aura or something and tell me about my spiritual level? I thought you psychics could do that sort of thing!"

Gently I persisted, "First, you must tell me what you mean when you say spiritual evolution. It's a vague term."

He thought for a minute, then blurted out, "Well, am I an evolved soul? How far upon the path have I come? Is this my last incarnation? You know!"

I do not know. I discussed the subject with him for a few minutes, trying to show him that he needed to clarify his ideas. Eventually he faded off to join a group of drinkers on the other side of the room. He did not appear to have gained anything from talking to me. No doubt if I had said, "Yes, you are a highly evolved soul", or, "No, your spiritual evolution has hardly yet begun", he would have been much more satisfied with our conversation.

Like most people who bandy about phrases such as "spiritual growth", he had no real idea of what he was asking. It is so easy to talk about spiritual matters without actually saying anything. Pseudo-occultists are always talking about old souls and young souls. Spirit guides are often said to be high souls but no-one ever admits to being a low soul. People seldom bother to define what all these terms mean, if, indeed, they mean anything. Often the use of these terms simply indicates an ego trip on the part of the person using them.

One of the funniest examples of this sort of thing that I have encountered concerned the "Doctor Johnathon" I mentioned before, who claimed to be an aura-reader. John was selling lottery tickets when I first met him but he gave this up to become a professional psychic. He advertised that he did aura-readings and past-life readings in slick brochures which used his new name, "Doctor Johnathon". Because the auras he read invariably revealed marvellous talents in their owners and since his past-life readings consistently included at least a couple of queens or emperors, John soon built up quite a clientele. Occasionally, when business was slow, he would put on a public demonstration. It was at one of these that I heard him give his personal views about "spiritual development".

The meeting was held in a suburban hall at eight o'clock one warm summer evening. When I arrived about 50 assorted women including a handful of little old ladies had gathered to hear the master. They were typical tearoom patrons, the sort who just love to have their fortunes told. I spotted a familiar face in the audience. He was Ivan Kroc, a well-known local figure in psychic circles. Ivan is a cynic; he is clever, humorous and interested in anything psychic. He loves collecting predictions from psychics and then calling on them afterward to tell them which predictions failed. He also makes notes on the claims of professional psychics and recalls these publicly should a psychic contradict a story told before. Naturally all the fake psychics find this disconcerting.

Doctor Johnathon knew Ivan also and decided he had better get the upper hand at once. As the meeting began, he spoke: "Good evening, friends. I see there are many advanced souls here tonight. Some of your auras are very bright. I see one . . . two . . . three people who have been around since Atlantean times." His gaze took in the audience and then settled on Ivan. "And, of course, there are also those whose souls are yet young and spiritually undeveloped."

Having put Ivan in his place, he went on with his speech. It was a long one, filled with flowery phrases and claims about the wonders of being psychic. Ivan did not say a word. But whenever Doctor Johnathon came up with something particularly outrageous, Ivan would sneeze. The audience soon realised what was happening and began to giggle whenever Ivan reached for his hankie. Poor Doctor Johnathon got redder and redder as the evening progressed. As long as he talked in an ordinary way, Ivan was silent. But the moment he slipped in anything boastful or pretentious, a loud sneeze split the air. Eventually the talk finished and he began to demonstrate aura-reading for people in the audience. Ivan was absolutely quiet except once when Doctor Johnathon told a 90-kilogram grandmother that she had great psychic potential. His whisper carried perfectly: "What, *her!*" His tone of utter disbelief evoked several sympathetic chuckles. After 15 more minutes Ivan stood up and walked out. He still had said nothing, but his silent withdrawal was an eloquent commentary on Doctor Johnathon's performance. The moment he was gone Doctor Johnathon interrupted the demonstration for some excited comments.

"Friends, far be it from me to speak ill of someone, but there has been amongst us one who is at a very, very low level of evolution. Spiritually, this one is on the lowest plane of all. The moment he came in I could see the darkness of his aura. I have never seen one so dark, so crude, with the spiritual light within so dim. Dear friends, a great weight has been lifted from our meeting since his departure".

Doctor Johnathon has no real aura-reading ability. Nevertheless, just this once I think he really believed what he was saying about Ivan's spiritual level. This sort of nonsense is still common whenever the subject of "spiritual evolution" is raised. People often assume that psychic development and spiritual development are synonymous — in fact they are far from being one and the same. Of the four or five genuinely spiritual people I've met in my life, none had any psychic powers. Conversely, at least two of the first-class psychics I know are thoroughly unpleasant people.

Every society has its stories of saints or holy people who possessed psychic powers. The Roman Catholic Church requires that any candidate for sainthood must demonstrate miraculous powers before being accepted. Since tales of holy people with supernatural abilities are found in every country and every age, we might conclude that there is some link between holiness and psychism. But what is it? Although many saints have supernatural powers, not everyone with supernatural powers is a saint. Failure to realise this has resulted in a good deal of confusion. I have noticed that the best psychics are commonly egotistical, which is hardly a saintly quality. Many are short-tempered, self-indulgent people. There is evidence that Adolf Hitler possessed excellent ESP but no-one has suggested that he was a saint. The method for psychic development given in this book does require certain attributes which correspond to the ideals of religion. Perseverance is one; optimism is another. Christianity lists joy as one of the seven cardinal virtues and, as I have pointed out, a cheerful attitude is almost a necessity for psychic development. Christianity also considers faith to be a virtue and this corresponds to the "believing" half of the believing–doubting tightrope. The doubting half might be compared to the Christian ideals of honesty or humility. The object of doubt is to help you avoid self-deception. So you can see that psychic development is quite comparable with a religious approach to life.

To a thinking person the existence of ESP proves that people are more than physical beings. If your mind can transcend time and space, there is obviously more to you than your physical body and its physical senses. ESP implies that a person's physical form is only the outer covering of something much greater within. In Chapter Four I discussed the view that the mind survives after the death of the physical body. We also learned something about reincarnation in Chapter Eight. The more you develop your psychic perception, the more you become aware that this lifetime is only a stepping stone along the path of your total unfoldment. In view of this, it is natural to wonder what life is really about.

Most philosophers have concluded that life is a training ground (or possibly a testing ground). If this is true, we should learn not just to succeed in life, but to prepare ourselves for something more. Most people who interest themselves in psychic matters come to this conclusion. No doubt that is why psychic development and spiritual development are often associated. Certainly an interest in one often leads to the other, but unfortunately, just as there is a lot of nonsense talked about ESP, there is a great deal of confusion as to what spiritual development really is.

My own opinion is that spiritual development means learning to be a decent human being. At any rate that seems to be the message of virtually all the founders of the world's great religions. To be kind and thoughtful, cheerful and productive, modest and diligent: these are the sort of characteristics that mark out the truly spiritual person. Being rich or clever or successful will not make you spiritual. Neither will developing your psychic powers add to your spiritual status. Learning to be a good person *is* being spiritual. It is as simple as that.

Do I hear you saying, "But don't spiritual people have to give up things? Don't I have to give up sex and smoking and all my material possessions?" It sounds like a remarkably difficult and uncomfortable thing to do, but people are always assuming that the spiritual path is a hard one. Fortunately, this is not the case. There is a path of meditation, the yoga of the mind as opposed to the yoga of the body, that can lead to spiritual growth. Although

it does require considerable effort, it is neither difficult nor
unpleasant. There are exercises that enable you to control all
negative thoughts or emotions, transmuting them into positive
ones. There are methods of elevating your consciousness to
higher levels. As in all things, there are right and wrong ways to
go about this. From my years of exploration I can show you some
real practical methods which actually work.

As a simple example consider the phenomenon of anger. We
have all experienced it. Everyone does things when angry, usually
only to regret them later — anger is a destructive, negative
emotion. Most thinking people soon realise this and many try to
overcome it by pure willpower. An untrained but determined
person who wants to conquer anger will grit his or her teeth and
say, "I will not be angry!". His or her face will go red, blood
pressure will rise and within a year he or she may have an ulcer.
The trained person does none of these. He or she learns not to
become angry in the first place. For this person, conquering anger
requires no effort, no willpower at all. He or she learns to stand
back from things which provoke anger with the result that anger
no longer affects him or her. Meditation is the key. There are
dozens, if not hundreds, of forms of meditation. Some are as
counter-productive as the so-called ESP development exercises.
Here are some meditative practices which I believe definitely do
work.

The simplest of all forms of meditation is one used to relieve
tension. It is a very easy method and completely infallible. Sit
down with your back straight and close your eyes. Decide how
long you want to meditate — 10 minutes is usually enough for
the first time. Listen to your breathing; do not try to control it or
to count the number of breaths you take. Instead, just say silently
the word "one" to yourself every time you breathe out — do not
actually speak the word aloud. Sit still, doing absolutely nothing
except to repeat "one" every time you breathe out.

Within 10 minutes your mental tensions will be gone and
much of your physical tension will have disappeared. Your pulse
will slow, your blood pressure will drop. Your whole body has
started to rejuvenate itself. When you stop, you will find yourself
calm and refreshed. The process is childishly simple, yet it works
like a charm. Practised as a regular exercise this can work
miracles for your whole being. It is the fundamental process
behind the famous Transcendental Meditation and it has been
proven to be remarkably effective. There is an entire book
devoted to this subject, entitled *The Relaxation Response*, by Dr
Herbert Benson. The book discusses the benefits of this form of
meditation; however, these few paragraphs tell you everything

you need to know in order to try it. The more you practise, the better the results. Scientific tests have shown that regular meditators become calmer, happier and healthier people after taking up the practice. Busy, tense people are usually unwilling to spend time meditating. Even if they try it, they seldom keep it up. Such people are precisely the ones who have the most need for meditation!

There is another exercise for tension which is often used in conjunction with meditation. It is a purely physical practice, very useful for those who suffer from muscular tension in the back, neck or any other part of the body. If you plan to do this exercise as a prelude to meditating you should sit with your back straight; if not, any comfortable sitting or lying position will do. Close your eyes and think about your toes. This may be harder than it sounds — how does anyone think about his or her toes? Try to feel them. See if you can feel each toe pressing against the next. Feel the pressure of your toes on the floor. If you are wearing shoes, feel each spot where the leather or sock touches your flesh. Make yourself aware of your toes. Then extend the awareness to the whole foot — sense your heel and instep in the same way as you did your toes.

Next imagine that your foot has become heavy. Think of it as being quite limp. Relax all the foot muscles so that your foot becomes just a relaxed lump on the end of your leg. Do this with both feet, then shift your attention to your ankles and the calves of your legs. The trick is to feel and sense each part of the body. Having done so, you can then relax the muscles of that area. Carry on, working your way up the body. Your knees will require special attention since there are always muscles pulling on the kneecap to keep it in place. The thighs are easy. When you have relaxed them spend a few moments imagining that each leg is now relaxed, limp and consequently heavy.

Next relax the pelvic muscles and those of the chest. Calming the chest will affect your breathing — you will find that your breath becomes slower and deeper as the relaxation is achieved. From here move the relaxation up to your shoulders: since the shoulders and upper back contain more muscular tension than any other part of the body, you must make a special effort to get rid of it. Then shift your attention to each arm in turn and continue the exercise. Move the relaxation to your neck and from there to your face. Work progressively up the small facial muscles, first around the mouth, then the cheeks, eyes and finally the forehead. The key to the whole process is to place your attention onto the part you are relaxing before trying to relax it. If you carry out this exercise systematically you will soon attain a deep state of relaxation. Do not try to take short cuts, you have to follow the method exactly for the full benefit. It is an excellent plan to use this exercise as a prelude to meditation. The combination of physical relaxation with alert concentration of the mind makes it ideal for that purpose. It is equally useful for getting rid of muscular tension at any time of the day.

The next exercise is not only a method for changing your state of consciousness, but also a way of stilling a restless or agitated mind. To understand it you need to know a little about occult psychology. If someone asked: "What are you?" you would likely reply by describing your job, your race or nationality or perhaps your beliefs. You might also mention your appearance, age, sex or personality. The real answer, however, is that you are a spirit. All those other things are simply ways by which you express your true self. We might call them clothes that your spirit wears. They are your outer garments. All your physical qualities are merely things you have built up during your lifetime, baggage you have collected along the way. Similarly both your thoughts and your emotions are no more the real you than is the colour of your hair. Your thoughts and your emotions grow and change throughout your life. Much as you may think that they are part of the "real you", they are only things you use, not things you are.

Sit quietly in the usual meditative position, eyes closed and back straight. Say to yourself, "My physical body is relaxed, but I am not my physical body". As you repeat this thought ensure that your body really is relaxed. Realise that the body is a tool you use to do whatever you want it to; it is your servant.

Next say to yourself, "My emotions are calm, but I am not my emotions". In doing so, take careful stock of your emotions. If you are in any way anxious, hurt or angry try to calm these things down. Soothe your own emotions. Like your physical body, your emotions are only your servant, not part of the "real you".

The third step is to say, "My thoughts are still, but I am not my thoughts". This is perhaps the hardest thing to understand, but it is true. Your thoughts can be speeded up or slowed down, they can be concentrated or scattered. They, too, are not part of the "real you". Relax them.

Finally say to yourself, "I am the immortal self". Hold onto this idea. The immortal self is you, the real you, your consciousness. It is the "you" that has just relaxed the body, emotions and thoughts. The boss, the one who is in charge of your physical form and your personality. Experience this awareness. For a few moments you will find yourself in a state of consciousness quite different from anything you normally experience. From this point, it is possible to do all sorts of things, some of which I will discuss in this chapter. First, however, some points on the nature of thoughts and concentration.

To realise that your thoughts are not you, but rather a tool which you use, is a very difficult task. One way to start is to sit quietly for a while and consider your own thoughts. Do you think in words or in pictures? Do you tend to repeat the same thought over and over? Most people do. Can you hold a single thought in your mind for a whole minute without something else popping in? Can you think of an item and then not think about it for five whole minutes? Block it out of your mind completely? Consider these things for a little while. Then try to turn off your thoughts completely — make your mind blank.

At first you will find that you can only do this for a few seconds. Nevertheless, the fact that you can do it at all proves that your thoughts are something you can control. The real you is the one who is able to turn your thoughts on or off. It is your consciousness. Now start to listen — listen to the noises around you. Try to pick out as many as you can. There are dozens of noises which you normally do not notice; see how many you can identify. As you listen to each sound turn off your thoughts: let the sound fill your mind instead of having thoughts and ideas there. You will discover that while it is usually impossible to keep your mind free from thoughts, by concentrating on sounds you can keep it free for minutes at a time.

There is no particular virtue in this practice, but it is certainly an interesting exercise. It will convince you more than anything else that your thoughts are not the real you, but only something that you use. Concentrating on sounds can be used as a stepping stone to other things, as learning to concentrate the mind is an important part of many types of mental training. In particular the western magical tradition lays stress on the twin arts of concentration and visualisation. You can practise concentrating on a visual symbol, a mantra or simply an idea. You can practise keeping a single thought in your mind by ensuring that every time your mind slips away (as it will be bound to) you bring it firmly back onto the subject again. With practice, you can learn to concentrate on anything for a very long time with absolute steadiness.

However, I am not convinced that this is a valuable thing to do. In my experience concentration for its own sake achieves nothing. To concentrate on something for a special reason is certainly justified, but to concentrate just for the sake of concentration is not productive. I have mentioned concentration simply as a way to understand that you are master of your own thoughts. But I do not recommend that you spend a lot of time on it. Once you have completed the exercise of calming your body, emotions and thoughts and have made the affirmation "I am the immortal self", you are ready for other meditative practices. I shall now discuss useful ways to extend the basic meditation exercise.

Visualisation is the process of imagining something as vividly and realistically as you can. It works best when you are properly prepared by being in a quiet place and going through the exercises I recommended. Visualisation can help you deal with all sorts of difficulties. Suppose you are facing a dilemma, say an important job interview, a sports competition or even a trip to the dentist. Prepare yourself first with the basic exercise. Then simply spend 10 minutes visualising yourself successfully encountering the difficulty. Picture yourself being strong and confident. Run through the whole scene in your mind, doing everything right, experiencing no problems. If you like you can repeat this process every day for a week. The result will be that when you come to actually approach the situation, you will have eliminated virtually all anxieties and probably improved your skill as well. The key to the process lies in running through the exercise of imagining success. Many people imagine difficult scenes over and over and consequently become more nervous as they do; that is worse than a waste of time. Controlled visualisation means imagining the scene positively so that it really is a success when you experience it.

The same process can be used to deal with bad habits. Do you want to stop smoking? Begin your meditation in the usual way, then spend 10 minutes imagining yourself going about your business without cigarettes. Imagine how healthy you feel. Imagine your pride at no longer needing or desiring to smoke. Imagine people congratulating you on your success. Imagine the sense of satisfaction in being a person who has beat the smoking habit. If you do this conscientiously it really will have a tremendous influence over your life. I must be honest and admit that the exercise is not 100 per cent successful. Nevertheless, it always has some effect on anyone who tries it, and for many people a few sessions of controlled visualisation are enough to completely overcome their smoking habit.

Are you easily angered? Visualise yourself doing the things that normally upset you, but picture yourself doing them calmly and quietly, without irritation. Is there a particular person who drives you crazy? Imagine that person pulling all his or her usual annoying tricks while you remain completely unaffected by them. This works, it really does!

The same technique can be used for health problems. There are now several institutions that treat terminal cancer patients with these methods. Although there are few cases of patients actually being cured, such patients do live longer than others and invariably enjoy greater comfort and peace of mind. Patients being treated for cancer and other diseases have found also that recovery is speeded up and facilitated by the regular use of meditation and visualisation. Imagine youself glowing with health. Imagine your complaint diminishing and your sense of well-being increasing by leaps and bounds. Ten minutes each day practising these visualisations will work wonders to help your condition. People under stress often suffer from psychosomatic complaints. These include backaches, skin diseases, asthmatic and sinus troubles, migraines, etcetera. It is very difficult to use visualisation to get rid of these illnesses once they have occurred, but it is simple to use visualisation to prevent them in the first place. One could liken this to trying to pour water back into a bucket once it has been tipped — it is almost impossible. But to stop the bucket from spilling takes no great effort.

Suppose you are a businessman who always develops 'flu before the monthly board meeting. Two weeks beforehand spend 10 minutes a day imagining yourself in glowing health, attending the meeting with no trace of a cold. I guarantee that if you do this exercise conscientiously you will have no symptoms on the day of the meeting. Once a cold starts, however, no amount of visualising will get rid of it. But with a little effort you can ensure it does not have a chance to start.

Virtually every type of human difficulty can be aided or eliminated through visualisation. Similarly all sorts of skills and abilities can be developed. However, I cannot stress too much that a conscientious effort must be made in order for the process to succeed. It is no good daydreaming while you are doing the dishes and then expecting the daydreams to turn into reality. You have to sit down, prepare yourself properly and devote time to the work.

As mentioned before, visualisation can be used in magic. However, my experience with people who have worked with magical visualisation convinces me that successes with this technique are few and far between. Every magician has stories of successes, but for every success there are a hundred or more failures. The reasons for this are complex, and are connected with karma (one's destiny) and the personality weaknesses that are usually associated with those who take up magic in the first place. There is not space to go into them here.

Apart from visualisation, another useful meditative process is contemplation, that is, contemplation from an impersonal standpoint. This is particularly valuable for dealing with emotional disturbances. By running through the physical/mental/ emotional relaxation exercise, you are dissociating yourself from many of the petty irritations of everyday life. Remember the final affirmation, "I am the immortal self". If you ever experience any sort of emotional problems, you can deal with them by doing this exercise and then by contemplating the problem impersonally.

For example, suppose you have a personal relationship problem. It could be something as acute as a marital break-up or as minor as a lack of romance in your life. Get into your meditative state, examine the problem and take it apart. Decide how many factors are at work and consider each of them in turn. Take each point and think it over. As you do so make an effort to "convince" yourself that it is not worth becoming emotional over the problem. This is a hard thing to explain but very important — the idea is not actually to convince yourself, not to brainwash yourself, but rather to reach a new level of understanding. Ninety-nine per cent of things that bother us are usually really not worth bothering about. The difficulty is in understanding this. In your meditation aim at reaching this understanding. Take each point and ask yourself, "Is it worth being annoyed (or angry, depressed, anxious) over this?" In the quiet of your meditation, look for a calm, dispassionate view of all the things that have been upsetting your emotions. You have already taken a major step towards calmness by affirming to yourself, "My emotions are quiet" and "My thoughts are still". This makes it easier to set about contemplating your problems with a view to taking the emotional sting out of them.

The technique will not actually solve any problem in terms of giving you an answer. It will, however, enable you to get rid of all or most of the associated emotional distress. In practice, by doing this you often do find answers because your state of mind has changed. An important factor here is to try to be positive or cheerful. Again, it is not a matter of repeating, "Everything is wonderful" in a desperate attempt to cheer yourself up. But while you are exercising the calm, dispassionate consideration, keep in mind that life is basically sweet. Even in the blackest moments there are always positive elements somewhere in your life. We lose track of them when problems arise but in your meditative state aim to look for them. The attitude is therefore more than a calm one — it should include optimism as well.

All these things may sound very difficult. Indeed, in the middle of an emotional crisis it may seem impossible to adjust your state of mind in this way. But if you set aside a time for meditation and carry out these steps in the meditative state, you will find that it *is* possible and extraordinarily beneficial. Try it. You will not regret it.

There is yet a third process besides visualisation and contemplation. It is a problem-solving method. As far as I know it has never been described in print before. If you have any type of problem, start by asking yourself what sort of solution you would like. Define in your own mind exactly what it is that you want to overcome the problem. Then go into the meditative state with this desire very clearly in mind. After you have made the usual affirmations, repeat to yourself just what it is you want. Now you must play a type of mental game: imagine that you are a spiritual being of great power and consider your desire from that being's point of view. You could imagine that you are a saint or a guru. Best of all, imagine that you are your own "higher self", that is, a powerful, wise consciousness, far above the petty "lower self" which deals with everyday affairs. You are now going to consider the thing that the "lower self" wants.

Suppose you are a student approaching an exam, and your desire is that you want to pass a certain test. Pretending to be your higher self, ask questions like: "Why do you want to pass? Do you deserve to pass? Have you worked hard? Are you prepared to make further efforts? Have you done everything you possibly could and, if not, are you willing to do so?" Now stop pretending and return to your normal self. Answer the questions as honestly as you can, clearly and sensibly. Imagine that you are addressing someone in authority whom you want to convince with the right answers. Next return to being the "higher self". You must be absolutely honest while examining the answers just given. Are they good or are there holes in them . . . factors your "lower self" really does not want to admit? If so, point them out as if you were a ruler reprimanding a subordinate. If necessary, repeat this process. Take the two points of view in turn, the "higher self" and the "lower self". If you try this you will find that it is impossible not to be honest. Somewhere in the process you will find the answers to your problem — it rarely fails. Do this as directed and you will almost always manage to sort out whatever is bothering you. Admittedly the answers you get may not be what you wanted in the first place. Nevertheless, they will be genuine answers. You see, what you have been doing in the "game" is shifting your own consciousness to a higher level, a level beyond the ordinary. By pretending to be the "higher self" you have actually lifted your ordinary consciousness up to that "higher self". There is only one "self", really, but most of the time we exist at the lower levels of that self.

Set out in a few paragraphs, this technique may not appear to be much. But like the exercises for developing ESP with tea-leaves, if you are prepared to do it you will be astounded by the results. Many occultists recommend the exercise of spending a few minutes each night reviewing the events of the day. This exercise is mentioned in so many books that I must comment on it.

Max Heindell, founder of the Rosicrucian Fellowship (no connection with AMORC) taught that this practice has an influence over one's destiny or karma. I do not agree. The purpose of reviewing the events of the day is to learn to stand back from them, not to remove their karmic influence. For example, if you made a mistake, review it with neither blame nor excuses. Do it with the objective of evaluating it. If you had a success, review it neither with pride nor pleasure, but with a calm evaluation of the incident. And if your day was full of things neither good nor bad, review them in the same way. From this practice you can learn awareness. You will also find that by doing so you are smoothing over many of the rough spots in your life. It is a slow process, but a useful one.

Many people who use meditation and visualisation like to spend time dwelling on things like love, happiness or kindness. There are many ways of doing this, ranging from visualising streams of affection flowing out from yourself towards others through to thinking kind thoughts about everything. If you play the "higher self" game you might also imagine yourself as a being of pure love and unselfishness. I have shown you how to play the "higher self" considering desire from a position of wisdom and fairness, so you might consider the same desire from the viewpoint of a loving parent rather than a stern teacher.

All the exercises described here will help you with your spiritual development. There are many books that will give you other methods — the religions of the world have produced thousands of them. Most, however, are clouded with the particular theological perspective of their authors. Of all the spiritual precepts I have encountered from religious books, I believe the wisest to be:

> Speak, so that whatever you say will cause no harm to anyone, and will be helpful or encouraging to those who hear you.

You might like to meditate on that for a while.

Throughout this book I have dealt with psychic phenomena, in particular with psychic powers. The development and use of such powers is an interesting and worthwhile experience. Nevertheless, what you have learned in this chapter will ultimately be far more valuable to you.

Chapter Ten

PSYCHIC READINGS AND PSYCHIC WORK AS A PROFESSION

The famous comedian Peter Sellers was a great fan of psychic readers. In fact he was addicted to them. Like many people he seemed to think that by visiting psychics he could somehow improve his tangled life. He ran from one reading to the next, always hoping that good news lay just around the corner. There is a story that he once courted a young woman who had just had a psychic reading. She had been told that the affair with Peter would not prosper, so she promptly broke off with him. Peter was furious. "Why didn't you ask me?" he shouted. "Just come along to *my* psychic and she'll tell you we're going to have a great relationship!"

Poor Peter! He thought it was just a matter of finding the right fortune-teller to make things turn out the way he wanted. An amazing number of people have this attitude. They go to a fortune-teller for good news, and if one psychic cannot provide it they go on to another. Over 95 per cent of a psychic's clients are there for exactly that reason. The remaining five per cent is made up of a mixture of people: some may be psychic researchers investigating ESP; others are ordinary people sent by friends rather than through personal curiosity; a few will be the sort of eccentrics always found when anything psychic is going on and then there are the lonely who just come to talk.

Very few people approach the psychic with a proper attitude of open-minded enquiry. In this chapter I propose to tell you exactly how to do this. You will learn how to avoid pitfalls and how to get the most out of a reading. Later in the chapter I shall tell you how you can actually take up psychic reading as a profession. If you have read this far and have carried out the exercises, your ESP is certainly strong enough to undertake professional work. Why not make some money this way?

When going for a reading the first step is to find a good psychic; this may be harder than it seems. The best method is to ask around among your friends or to phone a few Spiritualists or Theosophists to ask who is the best reader in town. People are always willing to talk about a psychic who has impressed them and personal recommendations are more reliable than advertisements. If you do decide to answer an advertisement, use plenty of discrimination. Do remember that dishonest and incompetent psychics always advertise widely and these adverts are the first ones you will see. Of course good psychics advertise, too. So how do you tell which is which? An ad that proclaims: "World's greatest psychic: guarantees to tell you everything with complete accuracy", usually masks a gypsy whose only ambition is to wheedle as much money out of you as possible. Also beware of advertisements in the classified sections that use the same words. These belong to the con artists who all use the same spiel to rope you in.

You can usually trust anyone who specifies the cost, particularly if the fee sounds reasonable (whereas con artists often advertise "free answers" or "questions only $1 each"). An advertiser also gains points for offering to tape-record his or her readings. Readers who can quote favourable press reviews in their ads are probably worth visiting. When you have compiled a few phone numbers, ring up to make an enquiry. It is sensible to ask: "What is the charge?", "How long is the reading?" and "What does it cover?". It is not polite to ask: "Are you any good?" or "How accurate are you?". A modest psychic will be insulted by the questions and a dishonest one will only lie to you. The answers to these first three basic questions will give a good idea of the person you are dealing with. If the psychic sounds competent, make an appointment. If you have several numbers, ring them all and then call back for a booking with the reader who impressed you most.

There is a right way and a wrong way to approach a psychic reader at your appointment. In the first place, you need to talk. Maintaining a stony silence is not the way to do things — it will antagonise the reader in the same way it would irritate an ordinary visitor. At the same time you must not chatter away and give clues to the reader. Make a little polite conversation. Let him or her know that you are friendly and interested, but do not give out any specific information about yourself. Above all, do not volunteer to tell the psychic what you want to know or why you are there. In Chapter Four it was pointed out that the sound of your voice can act as a psychic stimulus. This is another reason for talking, apart from the need to set up a pleasant, relaxed relationship with the psychic. Nevertheless, you should not talk so much that the psychic cannot get a word in. He or she should do the talking; your job is to be pleasant and responsive.

It is wise to be on your guard, but never be deceptive. Some people think it is clever to mislead a reader. In fact it is downright silly. Such people ask Spiritualists about nonexistent relatives, interrogate fortune-tellers on when they will marry when they are already married and pull similar deceptions. You have only yourself to blame if you mislead a psychic and get a muddled reading. It is possible to avoid giving clues without resorting to dishonesty.

You are entitled to ask questions, but the best time for this is at the middle or end of a reading, not at the beginning. Use general terms, for example, "Can you tell me anything about my job?" rather than, "Will my boss give me a raise next Thursday?". Be wary of readers who ask you questions — consciously or not, they are fishing for information. Take care to show a moderate interest in everything rather than ignoring part of the reading and showing excitement over other points. Fake readers watch your expression and listen to your voice to find out what you want to know and when they are getting warm. By all means ask a reader to elaborate on something that interests you, or tell the reader frankly when he or she is right or wrong. Just be careful about how you do it.

If a reader asks you something point-blank, answer with complete honesty. However, make a mental note of exactly what you said. An experienced fake reader will usually pass over what you tell him or her, then reintroduce it later in another form; remember this. Honest readers sometimes ask questions too. It is up to you to keep track of exactly what you have revealed so that afterwards you can sort out how much ESP has really been at work. The most sensible thing to do during a psychic reading is to record it on a tape-recorder. A few years ago these machines were a luxury, but now you can buy one for the price of a psychic reading. It is an invaluable tool when investigating seances, psychic readings, etcetera. A few psychics are unwilling to let you record their sessions, but most honest readers welcome it. Among those who object, the most common complaint is that neurotic clients tend to play their tape over and over and then keep ringing up to enquire what this or that phrase means. Such clients are prone to brooding over any hint of future troubles. I have known two psychics who find that tape-recorders always malfunction when brought into their presence. This is not as far-fetched as it may sound — there is evidence that delicate electronic machinery may be affected by the minds of those around; computers, teletype machines, electric typewriters and digital watches have all been cited at various times. It is wise to ask the psychic for permission to tape-record before your appointment. Some of the best readers include a tape-recording as part of their service. If you cannot get access to a tape-recorder you will have to content yourself with pen and paper. The correct technique is to jot down brief notes or key words while the reading is in progress. Rewrite them later in detail, as soon after the reading as possible — the longer you wait to transcribe, the more information will slip your memory. It is unwise to attempt detailed records while the reading is in progress. This will interfere with your attention and distract the reader.

There is also a right and a wrong time to go for a psychic reading. The wrong time is when you have a problem on your mind. Naturally this is exactly when most people decide to visit a reader. If you are worried or upset the psychic will usually pick this up and it will influence the reading. I have pointed out already how my tarot cards usually reflect the psychological state of the questioner. So, too, psychic readers are prone to reflecting the hopes, fears and dreams of their clients. Although it is actually the mark of a true psychic to tell you something relevant to the problem on your mind, unfortunately predictions the psychic gives often prove to be no more than an optimistic projection of that concern. This is not to accuse the psychic of fabricating. He or she is reporting what he or she picks up. Time after time this proves to be just what the worried client wants to hear. Perhaps Peter Sellers was not so far wrong when he stated that his psychic would predict a successful romance. Usually such predictions contain a proportion of accurate details which make them all the more believable. Often they are nothing more than wishful thinking.

You should not wait until your marriage breaks down, your house is repossessed or your dog contracts rabies before visiting a psychic. The best time is when your life is busy and there are no major problems in the offing — this gives the psychic something to work with. There are few things more disheartening to a reader than working for a client who has nothing happening in his or her life. If problems do loom ahead the chances are the psychic will perceive them and warn you what to do about them. If you keep a record of every reading you will always be able to check back when a problem does arise.

Once you have found a good psychic it is wise to visit him or her once or twice a year, assuming you want to have more than one reading. It is highly unwise to visit a psychic more often than this, except under special circumstances. Regular visits to a psychic, on a monthly or even weekly basis, are the height of foolishness for they foster an unhealthy dependence on the psychic. People who do this usually lose their ability to think and act for themselves. They commonly become neurotic, lose their initiative and can become so obsessed with the future that they lose contact with the present. However, neurotic people who go to psychics are prone to becoming addicted to them. It is an open question as to whether the neurosis caused the addiction or the addiction provoked the neurosis.

Frequent visits to a psychic also put a strain on the reader. He or she is under pressure to pick up something new at every session and often this is simply not possible. The psychic's mind becomes clouded with impressions and the facts he or she already knows about the client. As I have stated before, it is easiest to read for people you do not know at all. Reading accurately for those you know well is extremely difficult.

The exceptions to the above include the low-priced tearoom entertainers who deal in minor predictions looming a week or two ahead. These readers are happy to see you every week or so. Also there are a few specialist readers who offer advice on business, financial and related matters. Such readers work for a few clients who conduct complex and changeful affairs requiring constant advice and guidance. This is a very difficult field, worked only by a handful of psychics in the world. Such psychics are usually knowledgeable and intelligent as well as being psychic, and are listed as "consultants" rather than as psychics. They are very highly paid.

Some people like to visit a variety of psychics rather than staying with one good one. This may result in a bizarre psychic phenomenon which misleads many who encounter it. A prediction or psychic impression that crops up during a reading is liable to occur in your next reading by an entirely different psychic. Usually such repetitions consist of improbable events of a colourful nature. The repetition is thus much more impressive than if it concerned a mundane matter. Naturally the client thinks that it must be true since two psychics have predicted it! When the next psychic and the next come up with the same item the client is convinced that a remarkable confirmation has been achieved. All too often the marvellous prediction fails to materialise. What has happened here is that the prediction given originally has been psychically picked up by each ensuing reader. The client is literally carrying it around with him or her, without knowing it. Ray Stanford, author of *What Your Aura Tells Me*, once encountered a man who had with him the impression of a spirit guide. The man remarked that many psychics had described this guide before. Stanford, a perceptive man, noticed that the spirit form appeared to be flat and motionless, like a picture. It transpired that it was simply a picture from a book the man had noticed years before, but which had stuck in his memory and was now being picked up by every psychic who encountered him.

I have known of dozens of analogous situations, generally predictions of fame, money or brilliant marriages, all repeated by psychic after psychic and all completely false. By running from reader to reader you undoubtedly run the risk of picking up just such a thought form. Cynics may wonder whether this is simply due to the fact that some psychics use stock predictions which they repeat to most of their clients. This could scarcely account for the woman I knew who was told by several readers that her cousin would return from overseas with an amassed fortune. That was 10 years ago. She is still waiting for it! Another explanation might be that certain unscrupulous frauds pass information about their clients from one to another. Apart from the fact that very few fake psychics are sufficiently well organised to arrange such a thing, there would be no point in it unless a pay-off resulted. To my knowledge this has never been the case.

Researchers and curious folk may legitimately visit a number of readers in succession. Bored people who spend their days tripping from one reader to another are a different matter. About the only genuine prediction such people can expect to receive is: ''I see you going to visit a fortune-teller.'' If someone spends most of the time going to readers, how can they expect anything much to happen in their life?

Now that we have examined all the dos and don'ts of visiting the psychics, it is time to look at the other side of the coin. How does a person set up as a psychic reader? Once you have learned to use your ESP — and I would hope that all of you will at least attempt to do so — it is natural to wonder whether you can make money at it. You will hear it said that those who use their ESP to make money invariably lose the gift. Is there any truth in this?

Charging a fee for giving a psychic reading is *not* wrong and will not necessarily result in the loss of your ability. There is, however, a danger that the constant pressure of work will put a strain on the reader and result in some sort of breakdown. Furthermore, psychics whose ability is intermittent or not very strong (as is the case with most natural psychics, but not the case with those trained as I have directed) are in difficulty when they have to perform day after day. They start to rely more and more on non-psychic methods to give their reading with the result that their ESP does start to diminish. The theory that charging money for ESP is wrong is usually espoused by those who see it as a spiritual or holy gift. Many Spiritualists see it in this light. They are entitled to their opinion, but they should realise that their personal attitude to ESP is not necessarily shared by others. My own view is that ESP is in no sense a spiritual gift, but that, like any talent or ability, it may be used for spiritual or non-spiritual purposes as the owner decides.

Let us suppose that you have taken the plunge and decided to set up business as a psychic reader. The first and most important rule to remember is that although as a part-time business psychic reading is easy, profitable and fun, as a full-time concern it is difficult, nerve-racking and no way to make a living. This is a lesson that everyone learns after a year or two of professional work. Why not realise it right at the start? The part-time reader is free to work whenever he or she feels like it. Assuming the reader has a regular job, whatever is made by the readings is pure profit. Seeing only a few clients, he or she is not overworked, never becomes bored and can let the business build up or slack off. On the other hand the full-time professional must always work at a steady pace, maintain advertising and other publicity and can never afford to relax. This reader also finds that he or she is trapped by the work since, once it is taken up, re-entering the normal work force is extremely difficult (just try listing "psychic for two years" on your resumé for a prospective boss!).

I therefore recommend any aspiring reader to start with a small part-time practice. If it proves successful you can always build it up into a full-time profession later. My own experience is that part-time readers usually have more work than they can handle and often make a good deal of money out of it. Full-time readers tend to give up after a year or two, having been unable to take the pressure.

Before you set up it is a good idea to investigate the legal status of psychism. Everybody has an opinion, but few really know what they are talking about. You will hear all sorts of amazing stories if you ask around. Disregard them and look it up in a law book. Here are some untrue stories I have been told: "It's all right as long as you never predict death for anyone"; "You can only do it in a tea lounge where food is served"; "You have to get a licence"; "You can do it, providing you never advertise"; "Only the gypsies are allowed to do it"; "It's legal if you announce that it's for entertainment only". These are all just rumours, though the tellers were convinced they had the correct information. The actual law is often found under the Vagrants and Gaming Act. Your local librarian will help you locate this. Or you can hire a solicitor to do the work for you. Be sure to obtain a photocopy of the page that contains the reference to fortune-telling.

Perhaps you think that "fortune-telling" is not the same thing as a psychic reading. Unfortunately the law does not see it that way. If you find a law against fortune-telling in your area you can be sure that the courts will interpret this to cover palmistry, astrology, aura-reading, ESP and anything that in any way suggests you can foresee the future. However, you may find that no-one has been prosecuted for fortune-telling for many years despite the existence of the law prohibiting it. It is wise to use your discretion in such cases. In places where psychic work is tolerated the police usually adopt a policy of acting only when a fortune-teller tries to swindle the public. Another common state of affairs is for police to act only when a member of the public registers a complaint. Honest psychics have nothing to fear. There are states in America where ministers of religion are permitted to offer "psychic counselling" while all other sorts of psychic work are forbidden. For this reason many psychics send away to mail-order churches which will ordain you for a few dollars. *Fate* magazine and papers like the *National Enquirer* and *Rolling Stone* carry advertisements from such churches. A common dodge is for psychic readings to be offered "free" when a client purchases a small item or patronises a tearoom. I have been told by lawyers that such a defence would not stand up in court since the reading is really not free — it is available only to a purchaser.

The best place to set up business is in your own home. Renting an office is an unnecessary expense and should be considered only if your home is unsuitable for interviewing clients. Many of the best psychics in London work from tiny rooms, so do not feel discouraged if your place is not an impressive one in a well-heeled district. Psychic work is one of the very few fields in which a fancy address makes little difference. However, if you do work from home you need to get conveniently established. Be sure you have a room where you will be totally free from interruptions. You also need somewhere to put your clients' friends since an astonishing number of people will not go to a psychic unless they bring a friend. Every psychic will arrange his or her own system for seeing clients and it is rare to find two who do it in exactly the same way. Use your own taste and discretion. As soon as you are in business, people may start to pressure you to change: to make your readings longer or shorter, change the hours when available, do this, do not do that, etcetera. Give in to this at your own peril! However you decide to do your readings it is up to your clients to conform to your ways, but this does not mean you cannot be flexible. You are entitled to undertake anything you want. If you see a better way, then try it. Just be sure that it is you who calls the shots.

You must have a system of taking appointments that is clear and careful to avoid confusion. A telephone is virtually a necessity unless you hire an answering service. If you do not want to work from your home or an office investigate the possibility of setting up a booth or table at a local market, arcade or shop. Here you depend on attracting passers-by and you can dispense with taking advance bookings by telephone.

A third method is to offer psychic readings in the homes of

clients, assuming you have transport to get around town. Some psychics specialise in attending parties or they arrange for three or four clients to meet in the home of a friend where the readings take place. If you set up this sort of system be sure to investigate exactly where you will be working and under what conditions you will work. (People have an amazing ability to spring surprises on you when you go out to visit them.)

The only real necessity when you are working professionally is a stack of business cards. You simply must have a card printed, as this is your main method of proving that you are genuinely in business. Cards are not cheap but are an excellent investment. The more you have printed at one time, the less expensive it will be. Many beginners timidly order a few hundred cards, only to be on the phone reordering in no time at all. The part-time psychic can usually drum up business by passing cards round to friends, putting a small advertisement in the classified section of the local paper or sticking notices on shop windows or bulletin boards. The full-time worker, who depends on clients for a living, is in a much more demanding position.

Extensive advertising is virtually a necessity for the full-time reader and here there is a sad lesson to be learned: you can spend a fortune on advertising with little or no results. Beware of people who want to sell you advertising space on the back of tickets, pro-grammes, matchboxes or public transport, etcetera — such ads are usually a waste of time. Newspapers and magazines offer a better return for money than almost anything else, but obviously some are better than others. Women's magazines are generally most productive since all over the world more women than men go to psychic readers. This is an interesting fact, especially since it is true in every country, even in Asia where businessmen and politicians regularly consult fortune-tellers. The most profitable advertisement is a display one in your main daily paper. Of course such an advertisement will be expensive, but it will pay for itself many times more than small advertisements in the classified section. The latter are not without value, but they cannot match a good display ad for results.

Another good way to advertise is by getting free publicity in the press or on radio or television. One good television appearance or a favourable newspaper article can bring you clients for months. Remember, though, you cannot expect a favourable response unless you put on a good performance. Nothing looks sillier than a so-called psychic on television who cannot get anything right. On the other hand a few accurate psychic impressions will get you a return invitation and all the attention you want. One way to attract the media is to visit your local newspaper office, radio or television station and ask for an interview. Another is to mail out news releases giving details of your work as a psychic reader. There are books that give you detailed instructions on how to write a news release. The basic technique is to write up a sheet of information about yourself, including a photo to catch attention, and send copies of it to selected media people. Make a list of local shows that might be interested, such as talk shows which require guest speakers. Where possible, get the name of the programme director and address your envelope to him or her. You will need to make up new releases every few months. A response is more likely on your third or fourth mailing, so do not lose heart. Be sure to vary the release each time. Above all, be sure your releases are eye-catching, interesting and provocative. Keep them brief, and use letraset to create bold headings — make your release as professional-looking as possible.

The best medium for responses is the press — nothing beats a favourable newspaper article about yourself. Radio is next best and television makes a poor third. One would think that television would be the best exposure, but for a psychic this is just not so. There are various reasons for this — television viewing is passive so viewers are not accustomed to responding. Only the top programmes, or a series of repeat performances, ever generate much actual public response. Press reviews, however, are a two-edged sword. A good one is priceless, but a bad one is an embarrassment. Reporters often try to be smart or funny at the expense of whomever they are interviewing, particularly if the person seems a little strange (such as a psychic). Be sure to be as serious and sensible as you can. Always monitor very carefully what you say to reporters: they will ask you hundreds of questions and then print only the parts they want, not the parts you might have wanted them to publish. Once you have had a good write-up in a paper photocopy it for subsequent publicity. If you have more than one article make up a portfolio to show interested media people.

In some places there are magazines devoted to astrology or the occult and, with these, advertising becomes rather tricky. It is a good idea to put two or three expensive ads in these to get your name known and then maintain a small ad to let people know you are still around. This raises the question of the occult community, that is, the whole body of people in your area who take an interest in psychic and related matters. There are always a few people who visit every new psychic and you will have the chance to meet some of these people who form the occult community. There are often clubs, societies, public meetings and newsletters which circulate among such people. You may wish to have nothing to do with them. On the other hand you can become well known and increase your clientele by getting acquainted with them. The important thing is to avoid the bickering which so often occurs in groups. Do not join cliques, do not spread gossip about other psychics and keep on good terms with everybody. When you come across any frauds simply avoid them — do not make enemies if it can be avoided. There is a good deal of jealousy and pettiness as well as a great deal of mutual help, respect and cooperation among the occult community. It is wise to be as helpful and cooperative as you can and to avoid negativity like the plague.

For the professional psychic a proportion of the trade will be people who come back for more than one reading. Obviously if you can get a number of clients to visit you regularly you will have a steady business. It is a good idea to try to arrange this. However, remember what I have said about the frequency with which psychic readings should occur. Discourage people who want to depend on you as an emotional crutch for every little problem. By all means invite people to return, but do not pressure them to do so. It is dishonest and distasteful to act in that way.

Should you keep notes on the clients who come to see you? In one way this is wise, since it lets you refresh your memory about a client if he or she calls a second time. However, it raises the temptation to impress a client with the use of the notes you have made. If you do jot things down it is best to let the client know that you have consulted your files when he or she returns to you. Absolute honesty is vital in your work — the moment you practise any deception your psychic powers will start to wane. The reason is not because you are being punished or penalised for what you have done, but simply that ESP is a delicate thing which has to be treated carefully. By depending entirely on your ESP you will get results; by depending on trickery you will diminish your psychic perception.

There are obviously a number of ethical principles that need to be observed when doing readings. For example, you should always strive to be helpful. Try to ensure that everyone who visits you actually benefits from the experience. This does not mean you have to flatter or offer only glittering predictions for the future. Simply try to be kind; say whatever you believe to be true, but let your honesty be tempered with gentleness. When people start calling on you regularly, there is a temptation to treat your readings simply as a job. It is easy when some dull citizen arrives for a reading to fob him or her off with half an hour of uninteresting, low-grade ESP. That is not enough. People are coming to you because they need something which you can give. You owe it to them to give each one the best you can. It is equally tempting to fall back on "safe" statements, that is, generalisations, obvious facts or the sort of thing that can be applied to anybody. Many fortune-tellers fall into the habit of filling their readings with this sort of statement, intermingled with only occasional flashes of genuine ESP. You must resist this: treat every reading as a fresh experience, a new challenge, never as a routine, rather tedious chore to be finished as soon as possible.

An English astrologer once told me her own solution to these problems. "It may sound trite," she said, "but when someone enters I say to myself, 'Care about this person, and give your best'. I use this like a spell to get myself into the mood for a reading. It certainly helps me to be on the ball with all of them." I think this is an excellent idea. A momentary reminder to yourself before each reading will go a long way towards keeping you fresh.

Because psychic impressions are never as definite as things you perceive with the five senses, many clairvoyants state their impressions in the form of questions. They will ask, "Do you have three children?", rather than stating, "You have three children". This is a very dangerous habit to fall into. It encourages guessing and leads to the "fishing" process used by phonies. Almost every psychic uses this questioning method at some time or another. Discipline yourself to say, "I think so-and-so", whenever you are doubtful and are unwilling to make an emphatic statement, rather than asking the client, "Is it so-and-so?".

Professional psychic readings always include a number of predictions. From what we have seen in previous chapters you know that sensing the future is about as easy as sensing present conditions, but that predictions are never completely reliable. Bear that in mind when making them. It is wise to dwell on good news: obviously you must never make up a happy future just to please a client, but you can certainly play up anything positive you sense and play down the negative things. We all benefit from encouragement and you will be more popular if you can find pleasant things to talk about. Deal with any troubles you foresee by offering warnings or advice. Make your comments clear and crisp, but do not spend too long on these topics.

If a client wants to talk let him or her do so, but you should not encourage this. Fake psychics are always expert at getting clients to talk; honest psychics will do most of the talking themselves. There are clients who visit you only because they want someone to talk to and, if you get one of these, by all means let this person have his or her way. This type of client never hears what you say anyway. A good plan is to talk steadily yourself but to let the client speak up if he or she wishes. You will soon find out which clients want to talk to you and which are more interested in listening to what you have to say.

I recommend arranging your sessions so that questions are left to the end. A client should be able to question you on anything you say when you are actually talking, but major questions should be left to last. This has two advantages: first, it places the onus upon you to fill up the reading without questions to guide you, and this encourages you to use your own ESP. Second, a client's questions are often deceptive since they reflect the client's hopes or expectations which may not be at all what your ESP reveals. Psychics can easily be misled by clients who tell them what they want to know right at the beginning. Leave about 10 minutes at the end for the client to talk or ask questions.

Finally, remember the point I have made before in this book: there is always room to improve. No matter how good you become as a psychic reader it is always possible to do better. Ten years ago I discovered the way to awaken psychic perception. I think that we have lifted one tiny corner of what actually waits to be discovered. For you this book has been a voyage of discovery. For me it is an account of what has been discovered so far. For both of us the voyage has just begun.